PARALEGAL CAREER STARTER

D1402599

PARALEGAL
career starter

2nd edition

Jo Lynn Southard

with Lauren B. Starkey

LEARNINGEXPRESS

New York

Library of Congress Cataloging-in-Publication Data:
Starkey, Lauren B., 1962–
    Paralegal career starter / by Lauren B. Starkey.—2nd ed.
        p. cm.
    Rev. ed. of: Paralegal career starter / Jo Lynn Southard. 1998.
    ISBN 1-57685-398-5
    1. Legal assistants—Vocational guidance—United States. I. Southard, Jo Lynn.
    Paralegal career starter. II. Title.
    KF320.L4 S68 2002
    340'.023'73—dc21

                                                              2001038736

Printed in the United States of America
9 8 7 6 5 4 3 2 1
Second Edition

ISBN 1-57685-398-5

For more information or to place an order, contact LearningExpress at:
    900 Broadway
    Suite 604
    New York, NY 10003

Or visit us at:
    www.learnatest.com

Contents

Contents

Introduction

Why Enter the Paralegal Field?

PARALEGALS, ALSO known as legal assistants, interview and communicate with clients; locate and depose witnesses; compose letters and pleadings; assist with depositions and hearings; and conduct will executions and real estate closings. Indeed, paralegals perform any kind of legal work that is not the actual practice of law. By reading this book, you will learn how to join the ranks of those in this exciting and expanding career.

The terms "paralegal" and "legal assistant" are synonymous. Sometimes, situations, such as local court rules that allow a "legal assistant" to sit at the counsel table in a courtroom, determine which term is used. "Paralegal" seems to be growing in popularity and is the term generally used in this book.

But what is a paralegal? First, paralegals are professionals who have knowledge of legal concepts, gained either through work experience or education. Second, paralegals do many of the same things lawyers do, except presenting arguments to a court and giving legal advice. Third, lawyers and law firms, government agencies, corporations, and other organizations employ paralegals. Throughout this book, you will find details on the kind of work that paralegals do as a matter of course. If the law interests you, but you don't particularly care if you get to argue in court, and you enjoy attending to detailed work, you might prefer being a paralegal to being an attorney.

This book contains an extensive analysis of how to get the training you need to become a paralegal. There are hundreds of different paralegal training programs in the United States, representing a variety of perspectives of the profession. You will find out how to choose the right program, as well as the right school that offers that program. From scholarships to grants to loans, everything you need to know about how to find and apply for financial aid is also covered.

You will learn how to conduct a job search and improve your job searching skills to help land your first job after you complete your training. By following the advice in this book, you can find work in an interesting and rewarding profession that has been called "America's fastest growing" by the Department of Labor. Here's a preview of some of the things you will learn:

STEP 1: INVESTIGATE WHAT PARALEGALS DO

Paralegals work under the direct supervision of an attorney. Their duties can vary, depending on the practice of their employer, but all paralegals do what may be called legal background or preparatory work. This means they perform research, both in a library or on an online service, and through client and witness interviews. Paralegals also keep track of client files, making sure they are complete and that things are done on time. They often write the first draft of memos or briefs. In many instances, paralegals send out correspondence under their own names.

Some paralegals, who work for solo practitioners or in small offices, are generalists, who may perform their duties under the rubric of criminal law one day, real estate law another, and torts the next day. On the other hand, paralegals who work for the government or in very large law firms specialize in particular areas of the law. Paralegals who work in the legal department of a corporation specialize in the area of the law appropriate to the company (for example, insurance law), and also in employment and corporation law. See Chapter 1 for more information on the duties and specializations of paralegals.

STEP 2: DECIDE ON YOUR TRAINING

At a minimum, you will need a high school diploma or General Educational Development (GED) Diploma in order to attend a paralegal program; in some cases, you will need a bachelor's degree. There are over 800 paralegal training programs in the United States, ranging in length from a few months to four years. Some programs provide a general paralegal education, and some allow you to specialize. You will have to decide, based on a variety of factors, what kind of paralegal education you want, and where to pursue it.

Chapter 2 also gives you information about the various programs and what you can expect from them. It includes sample curricula from paralegal programs and information about accreditation. You will also learn about the different settings at which training programs are offered. Certification options and information on states that offer certification is included as well. Community colleges, business schools, and four-year institutions are examined, and a list of criteria is offered to help you determine which will best suit your needs.

STEP 3: PAY FOR YOUR TRAINING

Chapter 3 details the possibilities for financing your education, including loans, scholarships, and grants. You will find out the differences between each option, including eligibility, the application process, and how awards are given. You will find out about the forms you need, where to get them, how to fill them out, and where to send them. Also, you will get some tips for simplifying and surviving this process.

STEP 4: ATTEND A PARALEGAL PROGRAM AND GET THE MOST OUT OF YOUR CLASSES

When you attend a program, you will want to get everything you can out of it. Chapter 4 offers pointers on making the most of your training. You will learn about internships, succeeding in the classroom, and taking your exams. You will also find note-taking abbreviations that will not only help you in school, but will also help you communicate with attorneys once you begin working.

STEP 5: CONDUCT A JOB SEARCH

While you're still in school, you should begin thinking about job hunting. In Chapter 5 you will find information on conducting a job search. The information in this chapter helps you research the job market, and then find the jobs available through a variety of sources. It also covers networking, a way in which more and more people find an ideal position. Chapter 5 also covers the key job searching skills: resume and cover letter writing, and interviewing. By doing all three well, you will greatly improve your chances of landing the position you desire. Job-hunting can be difficult, but the hints in these chapters will help to ease your anxiety, handle the process in an organized and effective way, and come through with a good job.

STEP 6: SUCCEED IN YOUR NEW PROFESSION

Chapter 6 gives you information that you can use to make any paralegal job—especially your first one—go smoothly and successfully. It includes hazards that can appear in the legal workplace and how you can avoid them—or recover from one. This chapter also shows you how to fit into your new job and get along with your boss and coworkers. And you will learn the importance of having a mentor, how to go about finding one, and other ways that you can promote yourself.

Finally, use the resources listed in each chapter and in the appendices to find even more information about the paralegal profession, your education, and job search. Listen to the words of those already working as paralegals, found throughout this book. Whether you are just getting ready to graduate from high school or college; whether you are in the workforce and want a change of career, or are returning to work outside the home, the information in this book can help you enter the field of law as a paralegal. Good luck!

CHAPTER one

CHOOSING A CAREER AS A PARALEGAL

IN THIS chapter, you will get an overview of the paralegal profession. You will learn what makes a successful paralegal, what paralegals do, and where they work. Descriptions of many areas of specialization, including family, criminal, corporate, and real estate law are included here. You will also get advice from a number of those already working in the field. Finally, you will discover the specific strengths and skills necessary to become a successful paralegal.

FROM *PERRY* *Mason* to *L.A. Law* to *The Practice*, television has portrayed the legal field as only Hollywood can: It's non-stop excitement and drama. Many are lured to the field with these images in mind. But, although the real world of law is less glamorous than the media would have you think, it can be a great place to work, and provides a rewarding career choice. It employs hard-working individuals who must meet the needs of many clients. They are trained to have a thorough understanding of the law and to put their education into effective practice on a daily basis. In the past, attorneys did most if not all legal work, but the growing need for legal services during the past few decades has made it necessary for many lawyers to delegate a share of the workload to paralegals. In fact, the U.S. Department of Labor has reported for over twenty years that the paralegal profession is one of the fastest growing in the country.

In the early 1980s, the Department of Labor said that by the year 2000 there would be 100,000 paralegals. Their estimates were off a bit. By 1994, there were already 111,000 paralegals in the United States. Four years later, that number had grown to over 136,000. According to the U.S. Bureau of Labor Statistics, employment of paralegals should continue to grow much faster than average through the year 2008. Most of these jobs will be newly created positions as companies and law firms continue to learn about the benefits of adding paralegals to their staffs. Of course, as more paralegal jobs open up, more people will train for the career and enter the job market, meaning competition for available jobs will grow. This is one reason the training discussed in the next chapter is vital; if you want to become a paralegal, you will want the best possible training to be competitive.

WHAT IS A PARALEGAL?

Literally, the word "paralegal" contains the prefix "para," which is from the Greek and means "alongside." Thus, a paralegal is one who works alongside a legal professional. Paralegals are trained to do most of the tasks lawyers do, except for those involving the practice of law (for example, representing clients in court, giving legal opinions, setting legal fees). In the short time since the paralegal position has come into service—in the 1960s—the job has grown from mostly clerical to almost limitless in terms of duties and responsibilities. As the demand for legal services continues to grow, so does the need for lawyers to delegate more of their work to paralegals.

National paralegal associations, bar associations, state legislatures, and supreme courts have all been involved in defining the term *paralegal* (or "legal assistant," as the terms are interchangeable in the eyes of the law); as the field continues to grow, the definition grows with it. The National Federation of Paralegal Associations (NFPA) most recently defined a paralegal as:

A person qualified through education, training, or work experience to perform substantive legal work that requires knowledge of legal concepts and is customarily, but not exclusively, performed by a lawyer. This person may be retained or employed by a lawyer, law office, governmental agency, or other entity or may be authorized by administrative, statutory, or court authority to perform this work.

The American Bar Association restated an earlier definition in 1997. It concludes "a legal assistant or paralegal is a person qualified by education, training, or work experience who is employed or retained by a lawyer, law office, corporation, governmental agency, or other entity who performs specifically delegated substantive legal work for which a lawyer is responsible." Most state legislatures, when faced with the task of forming a definition, use that of the American Bar Association. The United States Supreme Court recognized the profession in a 1989 ruling: "It has frequently been recognized in the lower courts that paralegals are capable of carrying out many tasks, under the supervision of an attorney, that might otherwise be performed by a lawyer and billed at a higher rate." (*Missouri v. Jenkins*, 491 U.S. 274, S.Ct. At 2471–72 (1989)).

The Birth of the Profession

As mentioned earlier, the paralegal profession had its beginnings in the 1960s. As the need for legal services grew in the United States, so did the diversity of those seeking assistance. Two developments within the legal field sought to address these issues: the plain-language movement and the poverty law movement, which led to the establishment of the Legal Services Corporation.

The plain-language movement suggested that the written product of lawyers did not have to be full of "heretofore," "party of the first part," and other overblown language whose only purpose was to obscure the plain meaning of a document and make people feel that they had to have lawyers to handle even routine matters. The purpose of the plain-language movement was to get lawyers to begin writing documents in language that an average person could understand.

Legal Services Corporation is a nonprofit corporation that grew out of the 1960s poverty law movement. It was established by Congress in 1974 to address the needs of poor people who did not have access to legal advice when they needed it, thus leaving themselves vulnerable to those who could afford a lawyer. Legal Services deals with big discrimination cases, as well as represents tenants and spouses who would otherwise be unrepresented in legal proceedings.

The paralegal profession was born in the 1960s, during President Lyndon Johnson's "War on Poverty," as a way of providing basic legal assistance to the poor. Although unable to give legal advice, a paralegal could help clients fill out forms, prepare them for court appearances, maintain contact with them, and help attorneys prepare their case. A few attorneys, assisted by paralegals, could provide services to many more people than the lawyers would be able to handle alone. Originally, paralegals worked in public agencies charged with providing legal services to the poor. Over time, corporations and private attorneys began to see the benefit of employing paralegals in their practices as well; now, most paralegals work in large, private law firms. Initially, paralegals were trained on the job; in the 1970s, paralegal training programs began to appear. There are more than 800 distinct training programs, 200 of which are approved by the American Bar Association.

WHAT DO PARALEGALS DO?

Depending upon where you work, your duties as a paralegal can vary widely. If you work in a large law firm specializing in family law, your day will probably involve researching matrimonial and custodial case law, meeting with clients, maintaining a calendar of due dates for responsive pleadings, and preparing those pleadings. If you work in real estate law, you may conduct title searches, perform financial calculations, and draft documents such as deeds and permits. However, you will find in your training that there are typical tasks performed by most paralegals; your education will focus on strengthening the skills you will need to succeed at them.

Typical Duties

Here is a list of some of the more common duties of paralegals. For a more comprehensive list, log on to the California Alliance of Paralegal Association's website (www.caparalegal.org/duties.html), where you will find information grouped by various specialties within the legal field.

- ► Research: library, online, public records, medical, scientific
- ► Investigation: interview clients, witnesses, experts; on-site analysis
- ► Writing: draft memos, briefs, correspondence, interrogatories, pleadings
- ► Administration: index documents, digest documents, organize pleadings, organize trial exhibits, monitor tax and corporate filings
- ► Docket control: prepare discovery requests and responses; schedule depositions; notify clients, witnesses, and attorneys of trial dates; file motions and pleadings

The particulars of any paralegal job will also depend on your employer; paralegals work under the supervision of an attorney, so it is up to him or her to determine which tasks you will be assigned in any given case. As in any profession, different attorneys have different ways of working. You might find that you have a great deal of autonomy to handle a case, or your boss may prefer a team approach. Either way, a paralegal can do almost everything that an attorney can do.

No matter what kind of office you work in, there are a few things that you can count on if you decide to become a paralegal. First, the work will be interesting. When people come to a lawyer, it is because something has happened—or is going to happen—in their lives that they want help dealing with. For example, the first thing most of us would do if we were arrested is to hire an attorney. Then, we'd need to tell our side of the story. As a paralegal, you will likely attend the first meeting with this client, and hear it all. Less obvious legalities can be pretty interesting, too—for example, the reason why your client wants to cut someone out of a will or how one company is attempting a hostile takeover of another.

Second, the work will be varied. Even when you specialize in a particular area of the law, your clients will have an assortment of legal issues. In corporate law, for example, you may deal with companies that produce anything from apple cider to zoo enclosures.

Third, the work will be satisfying. While it is true that a lawyer can't solve every problem exactly the way a client wants it solved, in most cases you will end up with a client who is grateful for the work that you've done for them. Also, from your perspective, most of the tasks you work on have an end; a solution. When you begin researching a legal problem, you may feel as if it's brand new and no one ever faced it before. Then you usually find that the law has dealt with it and there is an answer. It can be very gratifying when you are the one who finds that answer.

Finally, as the paralegal profession continues to grow, you will be presented with more and more opportunities for growth within your career. Whether you take on more responsibility within a job or leave your job for a new paralegal job in another area of the law, you will be in charge of your own professional destiny. As the demand for paralegals grows throughout the country, it can even provide you with the opportunity to transfer to a new area—and easily find a job.

The Unauthorized Practice of Law

The unauthorized practice of law is undoubtedly the single most important consideration in your career, and can present difficulties, because it remains a fine, sometimes fluctuating, line. What constitutes the practice of law, or the unauthorized practice of law, is determined by each state's judicial branch. Therefore, the definition varies from state to state. It is vital that as a paralegal you are aware of what the definition of "practice of law" is in your state and take care that you don't do it. If a court determines that you have practiced law, you and your firm can be heavily fined. But how do you perform your job duties without ever crossing the line?

First, every time you communicate with a court, client, witness, or opposing counsel, make it clear that you are a paralegal and not an attorney. Second, never give advice about a legal matter. For example, paralegals frequently help clients fill out forms, such as tax, corporate, or bankruptcy forms. But as Claire Andrews, director of paralegal programs at Casco Bay College in Portland, Maine, notes:

> The dangerous part is [when helping clients with a bankruptcy,] they can easily step over into the unauthorized practice of law. Technically, what they should be doing is helping people fill out the forms. If they do something like help them decide whether they're going to file Chapter 15 or Chapter 11 [bankruptcy], they're practicing law.

In addition to state-to-state variations, the definition of the practice of law is continually evolving. To make things less clear, the practice of law is often defined in the negative. Someone (a paralegal, a real estate broker, a banker, a notary public, etc.) may undertake an activity that someone else perceives as the practice of law and, therefore, something that should be done by lawyers only. A complaint is made against that person, and eventually a court determines whether the activity is or is not the practice of law. Then, another activity is added to one side of the list or the other.

For example, the definition of *Unlicensed Practice of Law* according to the Florida Statutes is as follows:

> The unlicensed practice of law shall mean the practice of law, as prohibited by statute, court rule, and case law of the State of Florida. For purposes of this chapter, it shall not constitute the unlicensed practice of law for a nonlawyer to engage in limited oral communications to assist a person in the completion of blanks on a legal form approved by the Supreme Court of Florida. Oral communications by nonlawyers are restricted to those communications reasonably necessary to elicit factual information to complete the blanks on the form and inform the person how to file the form. (Florida Statutes, chapter 10-2.1(a).)

In other words, in any given situation, you must research the statutes, court rules, and case law of Florida to determine if a particular activity constitutes the practice of law.

If you are not an attorney and you want to engage in an activity that you think may constitute the practice of law, and there is no reference to it in the statutes, court rules, or case law, the rules regulating the Florida Bar allow you to request that the Standing Committee on Unlicensed Practice of Law give you an advisory opinion, indicating whether they believe the activity is the practice of law. The Supreme Court of Florida has the final word, however. This procedure is similar in other states. This issue is very important to the future of the paralegal profession and will continue to be high on the agenda of paralegal associations, bar associations, and paralegal educators.

Logging Hours on the Job

Firms of any size generate their income through billable hours. These are the actual hours of work that can be billed to a client, and they include only the time that the lawyers and paralegals spent working for that particular client. They don't include things like taking a break or learning how to unjam the copy machine. Working as a paralegal for a firm, you will have to keep track of your time and be accountable for it. Expectations vary from firm to firm across the country, but you should plan on billing between twenty-five and forty hours per week. In 2000, according to the National Association for Legal Assistants (NALA), billing for paralegals ranged from $52 to $83 per hour.

JOB SATISFACTION

As with any type of employment, job satisfaction can vary greatly among paralegals. Those with the greatest satisfaction are the ones who continue to grow professionally. They may participate in continuing education seminars, become involved in a professional organization, or seek certification from a national- or state-accredited certification program. These paralegals also seek out or ask for more complex work assignments. Note that all of these activities are proactive, generated by the paralegal—those with a desire to grow, and a willingness to find opportunity rather than wait for it to come to them, are the most satisfied with their jobs.

The factor responsible for the greatest sense of job dissatisfaction in the paralegal field is underutilization or improper utilization. Getting the right training, and going through a job search can seem pointless if you're hired by an attorney who assigns you only clerical tasks. If you're not using your paralegal skills and aren't given the chance to rise to a challenge, you may be ready to call it quits. However, as more and more attorneys learn what paralegals are and what they do, the likelihood of being underutilized is diminishing. A survey of over 3,000 paralegals, conducted in 2000 by the National Association for Legal Assistants notes that, of paralegals with five or more years of experience, 73% report an increase in their job responsibilities and duties over the course of their employment. Even with this good news, it's still a good idea to ask for a job description and speak to other paralegals working at a firm before accepting an offer of employment.

The National Federation of Paralegal Associations' 1999 survey showed that salaries and bonuses were also a source of job dissatisfaction. In Chapter 5, you will find out how to research paralegal compensation in your area. This is a critical step in the job search process, and can help you to avoid accepting a job where the benefits package will leave you dissatisfied.

SALARY AND BENEFITS

The same NFPA survey reported that in 1999 the average paralegal salary was $38,085. However, the earnings of paralegals can vary a great deal, depending on the level of education and experience of the paralegal and the geographic location and size and type of the employer. Throughout the country, paralegal salaries range from about $10,000 to over $80,000. As a rule, if you are in a large urban area and work for a large firm, you will make more than paralegals in smaller cities at smaller firms. The average annual salary of paralegals employed by the federal government is about $5,000 more than that earned by legal assistants in the private sector, but there are individual opportunities to make more in the private sector.

Paralegal benefits vary as well. Most receive vacation, sick leave, life insurance, and medical benefits. Less than half of paralegals have access to a pension plan, although most can participate in a 401K–type of savings plan. Paralegals who received a bonus (65% of those surveyed) reported that it averaged over $2,200.

A current issue in the paralegal profession is that of overtime. Most paralegals are nonexempt employees; that is, they must be paid overtime for working over 40 hours a week. Some paralegals would prefer to be exempt employees and paid a straight salary; they believe that nonexempt employees, because they are paid an hourly wage, are seen as less professional. Gayle Lund, a litigation paralegal in Los Angeles, notes:

> The paralegal associations are very involved in the dispute about whether we should be professionals and receive a straight salary or whether we should receive overtime. To me, overtime is unprofessional. You might have to sacrifice for a few years on a straight salary, but if you want to be respected as a professional, you need to be recognized as a professional, and that's one of the ways you do it.

WHAT MAKES A GOOD PARALEGAL?

While people from varied backgrounds with very different experiences and skills have become successful paralegals, there are some traits that all successful paralegals have in common. Good communication skills are at the top of the list; paralegals need to be able to communicate well, both orally and in writing. They are expected to attack problems in a logical and methodical way, and must be organized and flexible in their approach to their work assignments. Paralegals have to be able to work well as part of a team and also on their own.

Often, you will have to deal with the public as you perform your job. Even in large firms, it is often the paralegal who does the initial interview with a potential client. Working with the public takes courtesy and patience, but in a legal setting, it can sometimes take even more. For many of your clients, seeking out a lawyer is not a happy experience. They may have been arrested or sued; maybe they are getting divorced, or have been injured, or must file for bankruptcy. As a paralegal, you could be the first person your client talks to when he or she decides to seek help, so you will likely encounter hundreds of stressed-out people during your career.

Lawyers depend on paralegals to do much of the background work for any given client. This includes getting information from the client, researching the particular area of the law involved, preparing memos that keep the attorney informed of the progress in the case, maintaining the client's file, and making sure that all deadlines are met. Messing up in one of these areas is one of the worst things an attorney can do; if it's up to you to keep the lawyer on track, it becomes your nightmare, too.

Finally, it is imperative that a paralegal always behaves in an ethical manner. There are a variety of sources of ethical standards for paralegals. First of all, as we noted previously, every state defines the unauthorized practice of law, which is what paralegals must not do. In addition, many state legislatures or state bar associations have addressed the role of paralegals in the legal profession. Professional organizations, such as the National Association of Legal Assistants, address ethical issues. It is up to every working paralegal to keep abreast of all of the ethical concerns of the profession.

National Association of Legal Assistants Code of Ethics and Professional Responsibility

Canon 1

A legal assistant must not perform any of the duties that attorneys only may perform nor take any actions that attorneys may not take.

Canon 2

A legal assistant may perform any task that is properly delegated and supervised by an attorney, as long as the attorney is ultimately responsible to the client, maintains a direct relationship with the client, and assumes professional responsibility for the work product.

Canon 3

A legal assistant must not: (a) engage in, encourage, or contribute to any act which could constitute the unauthorized practice of law; and (b) establish attorney–client relationships, set fees, give legal opinions or advice, or represent a client before a court or agency unless so authorized by that court or agency; and (c) engage in conduct or take any action which would assist or involve the attorney in a violation of professional ethics or give the appearance of professional impropriety.

Canon 4

A legal assistant must use discretion and professional judgment commensurate with knowledge and experience but must not render independent legal judgment in place of an attorney. The services of an attorney are essential in the public interest whenever such legal judgment is required.

Canon 5

A legal assistant must disclose his or her status as a legal assistant at the outset of any professional relationship with a client, attorney, a court or administrative agency, or personnel thereof, or a member of the general public. A legal assistant must act prudently in determining the extent to which a client may be assisted without the presence of an attorney.

Canon 6

A legal assistant must strive to maintain integrity and a high degree of competency through education and training with respect to professional responsibility, local rules and practice, and through continuing education in substantive areas of law to better assist the legal profession in fulfilling its duty to provide legal service.

Canon 7

A legal assistant must protect the confidences of a client and must not violate any rule or statute now in effect or hereafter enacted controlling the doctrine of privileged communications between a client and an attorney.

Canon 8

A legal assistant must do all other things incidental, necessary, or expedient for the attainment of the ethics and responsibilities as defined by statute or rule of court.

Canon 9

A legal assistant's conduct is guided by bar associations' codes of professional responsibility and rules of professional conduct.

Copyright © 1997 NALA

THE IMPORTANCE OF TRAINING

Most people entering the paralegal field in the twenty-first century do so after obtaining formal paralegal training. According to the year 2000 NALA survey of paralegals already working in the profession, 72% reported that they had a college degree, and 80% said that they had completed some form of paralegal training program. There is a growing trend nationwide for employers to prefer those with a bachelor's degree; it may even become a standard requirement. Chapter 2 explains all you will need to know about paralegal education, from choosing the type of program, to finding the right school at which it is offered.

A paralegal training program won't just prepare you in the classroom—many offer or require an internship for their students. This is an excellent entrée into the profession. Many lawyers are hired by the firm where they interned, and the same is true for paralegals. After all, firms don't take on an intern unless they have some work that needs to be done, and the internship period allows them to see if they like you and you like them before either of you contemplate making the arrangement permanent. And even if your internship doesn't result in a job offer, or you decide to decline the offer, an internship provides valuable experience that will help get you your first job.

Most paralegals who don't get their first job through an internship hear about openings through their paralegal school's placement program. The placement office is an invaluable job search resource, which may offer everything from help with resume writing and interview skills to setting up interviews with hiring firms. Many placement offices have relationships with employers who routinely hire graduating paralegals, and who recruit on campus to fill job openings. Chapters 2 and 4 have much more information about placement programs.

SPECIALIZATION

The area of the law you work in may depend largely on the specialty of your employer. In a small general practice firm, the area of the law depends on the problems of the clients who come through the door. Was your client arrested? Then you will be researching criminal law. Does your client want a divorce? Then you will need to know family law. A will? Estate planning and probate. For many in the field, that's what makes the law interesting; others prefer to become specialists in one or two of these areas.

Your background may also dictate a specialty. If you already have work experience in a particular field that you've enjoyed, you can include corresponding study during your training in order to set yourself up to specialize. Do you have any medical training or experience? You might be perfect for a law office that represents a lot of medical malpractice cases, especially if you've been trained in tort law. Penny, a career counselor with the Affiliates (a nationwide legal placement service) in Houston, Texas, says,

> [Medical malpractice] is a market that doesn't seem to have a lot of competition in it. For example, take registered nurses who have litigation experience—not necessarily practicing nurses, but people who do litigation and have an RN—we have a lot of those types of positions open that we can't fill.

Do you have experience or training in social work or education? Perhaps you will be drawn to family law. You will want to take courses in this area in order to make the most of your experience once you begin working.

Common specialty areas include administrative law, family law, civil litigation, bankruptcy, corporate and business law, criminal law and procedure, intellectual property, estate planning and probate, and real estate law. Other specialty areas, such as environmental law, will continue to grow but are currently less common. There are many other areas that are very specialized and limited to rather small numbers of law firms, such as Native American law or education law. A few of the most common areas of specialization are the focus of the next section.

Administrative Law

Administrative law refers to the law that is generated by governmental administrative agencies. Although these agencies may fall under the legislative branch of the federal, state, or local government, most of them are under the rubric of the executive (the president, governor, or mayor) branch. They may be in federal or state government and vary from state to state, but include the Social Security Administration, the Internal Revenue Service, and, in states, such areas as education and worker's compensation. In addition, more and more cities have human rights boards that deal with discrimination issues within the city. Specializing in this area may allow paralegals to represent clients in adversarial settings before administrative law judges, because in many cases petitioners may be represented by anyone they choose; it need not be a lawyer.

Family Law

Family law deals with divorce, child custody and support, and adoption. This can be a very rewarding area of the law, but it can also be quite stressful. Many who specialize in this area have very strong political beliefs (about the rights of women or children, for example) that impel them to work in family law, where they feel they can make a difference. For many firms, especially small ones, family law is the real bread-and-butter of the business. As a paralegal in family law, you will draft divorce and child custody petitions, gather financial and asset information, and spend a lot of time with clients.

Civil Litigation

Litigation involves lawsuits and the possibility of court battles, although most lawsuits are settled before reaching trial. "Civil" refers to the areas of the law that are not criminal—that is, disagreements between parties that do not involve the police power of the state. By definition, this area deals with disputes—one side trying to prove it is right and that the other side is wrong. To be successful in this area, you need to be flexible; you may be on a side you don't personally believe in, but you must zealously represent your client. You also need to be organized and detail oriented. For example, clients can lose cases because their attorneys failed, for example, to file a response on time. This also opens the offending lawyer up to a malpractice suit. As a litigation paralegal, you will be responsible for, among other things, keeping track of dates and deadlines. You will also conduct investigations and witness interviews. When a case goes to court, you may be asked to go as well.

Bankruptcy

Bankruptcy, often called debtor–creditor law, is becoming a desirable specialty, in part because it can be very lucrative. In the past few decades, the number of bankruptcies has increased greatly. This used to be an indicator of a weak economy; that is, when the economy was bad, bankruptcies increased.

Recently, though, even with a good economy, people seem to continue to get into too much debt, and bankruptcies continue to grow in number.

As a paralegal, you may work for an attorney who represents debtors, creditors, or trustees. Obviously, debtors are the ones who owe the money, and for them you will gather together financial information, draft the bankruptcy petition, prepare the schedule of assets and liabilities, and file any periodic reports. If you work for the person to whom the money is owed—the creditor—you will draft and file the proof of claim. If you work for a trustee (who may or may not be a lawyer), you will notify all parties who might have claims, track any transfers or payments of assets, and review claims. Unlike most areas of the law, bankruptcy can be handled by a paralegal from beginning to end, except for the decision to file and the decision about which chapter to file. There is very little "practicing of law" in bankruptcy.

Corporate and Business Law

Although many paralegals work for corporations, not all of them practice corporate law. For example, paralegals who work for an insurance company and deal with customer claims are working in insurance law. These paralegals are sometimes called corporate but are more appropriately labeled in-house legal department paralegals. On the other hand, corporate law deals with business transactions, incorporations, mergers and acquisitions, and ongoing corporate matters. These include drafting or amending articles of incorporation or bylaws; drafting shareholders' agreements and stock options; and preparing meeting agendas, notifying meeting participants, and taking meeting minutes. Corporate law paralegals may work in a law firm, corporation, government agency, or non-profit organization.

Criminal Law

Criminal law involves violations of the rules of society, such as drunk driving or assault. Criminal procedure involves constitutional law, in the form of the Fourth Amendment to the U.S. Constitution, which states, "The right of the people to be secure in their persons, houses, papers, and effects, against unreasonable searches and seizures, shall not be violated, and no warrants shall issue, but upon probable cause, supported by Oath or affirmation, and particularly describing the place to be searched, and the persons or things to be seized."

Paralegals specializing in criminal law may conduct fact investigations, perform legal research, prepare a client and possible witnesses for depositions, and prepare for trial. On occasion, the people and situations in criminal law and procedure are a bit unsavory, but the work is always interesting. And nothing is more important in our society than protecting individual constitutional rights.

Intellectual Property

The practice area of intellectual property involves protecting the creations, ideas, and inventions of people and businesses. This area of the law deals with trademarks, which protect manufacturers' rights to the identification of their products; patents, which protect inventors' rights to make and market their inventions; copyrights, which protect the products of authors and artists; and trade secrets law, which deals with a company's right to keep secret formulas, designs, and other information that gives them a competitive advantage. Intellectual property deals with the property that results from using one's intellect.

This is a very specialized area of the law; in fact, lawyers who work in this area are members of a distinct bar. The advent of computers and all the software that goes with them has made this a very hot and fast-growing field.

Estate Planning and Probate

Like bankruptcy, many paralegals are attracted to estate planning and probate because it is a field in which they can work independently. Estate planning involves helping clients utilize procedures—such as the creation of trusts—that allow them to bequeath their property without having to go through probate. Probate is the legal procedure by which a deceased person's property is located and distributed. If the decedent had a will, it is called a testate proceeding; if there is no will, it is an intestate proceeding, and state law will determine how the person's property is disbursed. Conservatorships and guardianships are also under the purview of the probate courts. A conservator is appointed to care for an adult who is deemed to be incompetent. A guardian does the same thing for a child.

Estate planning in particular requires knowledge of accounting procedures and investments, as well as the law of trusts and estates. For paralegals who have this knowledge, there is a great deal of autonomy in the field; there are even times when you can appear in court on behalf of a client.

Real Estate

Real estate law is another field that allows paralegals to work autonomously. This area involves representing buyers and sellers of residential or commercial property, lenders or borrowers for the financing of these sales, and landlords or tenants. To do this, paralegals deal with titles, the documents that give possession of property to a particular owner, and also with any rights that others may have to the property (through a lien or lease, for example). Titles must be thoroughly searched in order for a sale of real estate to commence.

Once the title is clear and the sale is ready to take place, paralegals are often responsible for seeing that the closing of the sale goes smoothly. This involves drafting any documents needed, such as mortgages, deeds, or bills of sale; estimating what the closing will cost; and managing the documents for the title company. A great deal of this work can be done by a paralegal with only minimal supervision from an attorney.

Other Areas of Specialization

If you decide to pursue a career as a paralegal, you will learn during your training that the law touches nearly every aspect of our lives. Thus, almost any subject can conceivably be a specialty area of the law. In addition to the areas described above, others include:

AIDS law

agriculture law

alternative dispute mediation (ADR—also known as mediation)

animal rights law

antitrust law

civil rights law

computer and Internet law

elder law

entertainment law

environmental law

employment law

human rights law

immigration law

labor law

legal malpractice law

medical malpractice law

Native American law

personal injury law

private (business) international law

sports law

WHERE DO PARALEGALS WORK?

Most paralegals work in private law firms. However, law firms may be comprised of a few lawyers or several hundred. Paralegals also work for corporations, the government, nonprofit employers, and a variety of other places. Almost every agency of the federal government employs legal assistants; the majority of them are at the Departments of Justice, Treasury, Interior, and Health and Human Services. Many state and local government departments employ paralegals as well.

Where you work has a large impact on what kind of work you do. The specialty of the firm or agency will determine your specialty. In addition, different workplaces have different cultures. The local Legal Service Corporation office or environmental action group will no doubt offer a much more casual work atmosphere than a large firm or a court. Keep the different kinds of work settings in mind as you embark on your paralegal career.

The Large Firm

The relative size of a large law firm depends on the city in which it is located. In Chicago, for example, a 100-lawyer firm is probably considered medium-size, while in Springfield, Illinois, that same firm would be large indeed. Baker & McKenzie in Chicago claims to be the world's largest law firm, with over 2,300 lawyers. (But those lawyers are divided among dozens of offices world-wide; the largest is the Chicago office, with over 180 attorneys.) In most places, however, a firm with more than 100 lawyers is considered a large firm. In some large law firms, there are more paralegals than lawyers!

Large law firms are generally divided up into departments, such as litigation, probate and estate planning, corporate and business organizations, and international law. This specialization allows the paralegals who work for these firms to specialize as well. A large firm may also contain a structured paralegal "department" that doesn't affect the specialization of the work you do, but rather provides you with a paralegal supervisor and, possibly, paralegal assistants. This structure also means that usually there will be an in-house training program and regular staff meetings. All of this can be very helpful, both in keeping you apprised of the latest developments in the firm and in the law, and in providing an intermediary between you and management. This structure also provides you with opportunity for advancement as a paralegal.

The attorneys in large firms are partners (there may be senior and junior partners) or associates. Associates are usually hired right out of law school, although they may have clerked for a judge for a year or two before joining the firm. After a period of time (often seven years), associates may be made partners or asked to seek employment elsewhere. However, some firms retain associates for much longer, without an expectation of partnership.

Generally speaking, paralegal training is more practical than law school. Even as a newly hired paralegal, you may find you know more useful legal information than your recently graduated associate boss. As Audrey Casey, chair of the paralegal studies department at Andover College in Portland, Maine, notes, "I've worked with attorneys who say, 'I know everything there is to know about a complaint, but how do you do one?' " This can create an uncomfortable situation in which you know more than your boss. In order to avoid a clash, it's important to remember that you are the support person, and maintain your professional attitude.

The stereotype of large firms is that they tend to be stuffy. Traditionally, the largest firms have been considered the slowest to change: the slowest to hire women associates, for example, and the last to consider changing their workplace conditions to meet the needs of their employees. Large firms tend to be more hierarchical and structured; they are places where things are done a certain way because that's how they have always been done. If you're looking for a workplace that offers some flexibility, a large firm might not be for you.

Large firms offer many advantages as well. First, the salaries they pay paralegals are among the highest. They also may be more willing to hire new graduates, since there will be other paralegals at the firm who can train and mentor them. Large firms have more resources than smaller firms. Their in-house library will probably be comprehensive, and they will have access to a variety of the latest technology in research. The computers in a large firm are more apt to be state-of-the-art than in smaller firms. These advantages can add up to an environment that is well suited to a recently graduated paralegal.

Sample Job Advertisements

Entry Level

Recent graduate with top credentials, 3.5 GPA or better, sought for international trade paralegal position. Great firm. Lots of responsibility. Immediate need. Salary $32,000.

Litigation Paralegal

If you're looking for interesting work, competitive salary and benefits, and a reputable firm, then this could be the position for you. Well-known, prestigious legal firm is aggressively seeking a paralegal who demonstrates professionalism, critical thinking, and attention to detail. Applicant must have experience in litigation and be proficient in Word and WordPerfect. Will be responsible for litigation research, detailed analysis, and other tasks as required. Salary $35K–$38K plus benefits.

Intellectual Property

Unique opportunity due to growth to join the Intellectual Property department of a large city law firm. Candidate will be working closely with two paralegals and will be responsible for supporting a team of attorneys who specialize in patent litigation. The ideal applicant will have paralegal certificate and/or bachelor's degree along with one year of intellectual property experience from a law firm or corporate legal department. Salary to $40,000 year.

The Small- to Medium-Sized Firm

When you work in a small- to medium-sized firm, expect to find an environment that is more relaxed and open to change than that of a large firm. These firms tend to be less mired in "old-boy" conservative traditions, and can be more flexible when it comes to things like their employees' childcare concerns, job-sharing, and even flextime work schedules. Another plus is, if you've begun job hunting and are still unsure whether you want to specialize or in what area you want to specialize, working in a small- to medium-sized firm will give you the opportunity to dabble in many different areas of the law. Although some smaller firms, and even solo practitioners, specialize, most are general practitioners. And even if they do specialize, they often supplement that work with an extensive general practice. This includes criminal law, family law, and real estate and probate work.

In addition to variety in the areas of law practiced, there is also variety in the work assigned to people who work in smaller firms, including the attorneys, paralegals, and secretaries. When there is a lot of business, everyone has to be willing to pitch in to run the copy machine. When it's quieter, everyone can afford to stick to his or her own job descriptions more closely. As a result, a paralegal in this setting may easily become an important and trusted member of a team rather than just one among many paralegals in a large firm.

However, there is also the possibility of getting stuck doing mostly clerical tasks. Not all attorneys are really aware of the differences between paralegals and legal secretaries, and many of them can't afford to have the clerical staff they'd like. Litigation paralegal Gayle Lund says, "Smaller law firms, maybe five- or ten-partner firms or sole practitioners . . . rely a lot on their legal secretaries to perform what are really paralegal duties." On the other hand, career counselor Penny says, "It's not at all mostly larger firms that are hiring paralegals, [but] when you get to the smaller firms, a lot of times you will see secretary/paralegal jobs. It can be advantageous to go to a small firm because you get a lot of paralegal skills; even though your title is legal secretary, you're really doing paralegal work."

On the down side, smaller firms usually have fewer resources. This means that their law library may be quite small, and you may have to go to the local law school or courthouse to do your research. Computer research possibilities may be limited, or nonexistent. Before taking a job with a smaller law firm, be sure to understand what will be expected of you; ask for a job description during your interview, and look around while you're there to see who is doing what.

Sample Job Advertisements

Real Estate Paralegal

Busy law firm with 25 attorneys is looking for a full time Real Estate paralegal who is highly organized and has excellent communication skills. The successful candidate will have 2–3 years of related experience. Our firm offers a competitive salary, excellent benefits, friendly environment, and pleasant working conditions. Flexible time will be considered.

Bankruptcy/Commercial Paralegal

Small firm needs paralegal experienced in debtors' and creditors' bankruptcy, as well as contract disputes and transactional law. Duties will include preparing schedules, pleadings, and preparing corporate documents. Must have experience in commercial litigation, bankruptcy, and corporate work. Salary is commensurate with experience.

Trust/Estate Paralegal

A mid-sized law firm is seeking a skilled Estate Planning Paralegal with at least five years of estate planning experience. The perfect candidate will have in-depth, working knowledge of estate and trust administration, deeds and trusts and trust and probate accounting. Legal writing and research skills are also a must. Experience is a plus. Salary up to $75,000 for the right candidate.

Corporations

When you're employed with the in-house legal department of a corporation, you will deal with corporate law as well as the law of the specific industry you are in. On the corporate side, you may assist attorneys with employee contracts and benefit plans, shareholder agreements, and stock option plans. You may send notices of meetings and take minutes at those meetings.

In addition, you will work in the area of the law that relates to your corporation. It is the responsibility of the legal department to stay on top of all the government regulations that relate to your business, such as antitrust, environmental, and equal employment opportunity, as well as any rules that relate more directly to your industry, such as banking or insurance regulations. If your corporation employs inventors or engineers, you will gain exposure to intellectual property law, and learn how to complete and file patent applications. Most in-house legal departments are too small to handle all of the legal issues that arise, so in some cases you will be working with outside counsel.

When you work as a paralegal for a corporation, the company is your one and only client. Many paralegals with families like this aspect of the job, because it means their hours are more regular than those of paralegals employed in other settings. Although unusual things can always happen if there is a lawsuit under way, expect to work nine-to-five, 40 hours a week, most of the time.

A downside to work in a corporation is that you will have less variety in your workday than if you had several clients in a law firm. Some people find that it becomes boring after a while. On the other hand, it allows you to become an expert in a particular area of the law, such as banking, insurance or manufacturing. If you feel after a few years that you are ready to move on, you will be in a position to present yourself as an expert, which can enhance your job possibilities.

A new trend in small corporations is to have a "legal department" that consists only of a paralegal. Often, the legal assistant will work in human resources or as an assistant to one of the higher-ranking officers. Many companies don't need an attorney for their day-to-day business, but do have some legal needs that can be taken care of by a paralegal. Taking the minutes at a board meeting, for example, does not require a lawyer. When a lawyer is needed, it may be cheaper for the company to hire outside counsel to do the final version of the work. So the paralegal can, for example, draft an employment agreement that fits the needs of the business, and an outside attorney can verify the legal points. Paralegals in these kinds of positions are also responsible for recognizing when outside counsel is needed.

The title of such jobs may not always be paralegal or legal assistant. It may be something like "special assistant to the president" or "human resources specialist." You need to look closely at the job description to realize that the job requires someone with paralegal training.

Sample Job Advertisements

Commercial Loan Closer

Freedom from the office! Travel to three networked banks to do commercial loan closings. Employer needs detail-oriented professional to report directly to bank president. This position requires you to have a car for travel. Employer pays mileage and parking. Terrific position for team-oriented person interested in banking! Good benefits plus FREE checking and other bank perks.

Corporate Litigation Paralegal

Paralegal needed to coordinate and manage the litigation docket for a Fortune 500 corporation. Duties include assisting the company's attorneys in the discovery process, preparing pleadings, investigating claims, assisting in settlement negotiations, communicating with outside counsel, etc. Must have bachelor's degree; paralegal certificate preferred. Must have substantial experience as a litigation paralegal with a corporation or large law firm and be a professional who can communicate with personnel at all levels throughout this large company. Computer proficiency a necessity.

In-House Securities Paralegal

Junior to Mid-level Securities Paralegal to work for terrific, high-profile investment company. Handle all state and federal securities filings as well as related corporate work. Great work environment and benefits. Pay to $45K. Requires at least one year of experience as a securities paralegal with a major law firm or corporation. Must have an undergraduate degree. If you are interested and have the required qualifications, please e-mail your resume.

Government

If you work for the government, the kinds of duties and responsibilities you have will depend on what department or agency you work for. Some possibilities include the Department of Justice, the Department of the Interior, the Environmental Protection Agency, the Internal Revenue Service, and the Immigration and Naturalization Service. Many of these agencies have state corollaries, although the names may be different. In addition to all of the departments and agencies, there are the court systems, both federal and state. There, you could work in the offices of the district attorney or public defender. In the courts themselves, there are positions such as court administrator, which involves managing the court's docket and personnel and perhaps conducting research for the judge. Other government positions that may not use the term paralegal or legal assistant in the title include export compliance specialist, who investigates commodities and data being exported outside the United States, and patent examiner, who assists in determining if certain inventions are eligible for patent.

Working for the government provides great job security and other benefits. In the legal field, the pay usually starts out higher than in the private sector but caps at a lower level. Finding and landing a government job is different than the process for civilian jobs. Federal jobs are rated using a General Schedule, which establishes salary rates throughout the government. The ratings range from GS-1 through GS-16. In addition, jobs are classified by occupational group; legal and related jobs are GS-0900. Read more about the procedures for government employment in Chapter 4.

Sample Job Advertisements

Paralegal Specialist, GS-950-7

Salary range: $26,897 to $52,675. Tax division, Department of Justice, various sections (civil, appellate, and criminal), Washington, DC. Duties: The incumbent will aid attorneys in litigating civil and criminal cases, including conducting investigations, preparing cases for trial, and providing legal advice and assistance. The incumbent is responsible for conducting factual and legal research; collecting, analyzing, and evaluating information; drafting reports, memoranda, pleadings, and correspondence; interviewing persons and preparing interview reports; analyzing documents, organizing material, and preparing synopses; summarizing transcripts; preparing charts and exhibits; and verifying citations and legal references. Qualifications: For GS-7: Applicants must have one full academic year of graduate-level education or law school or superior academic achievement or one year of specialized experience equivalent to the GS-5 level. Nonstatus candidates at the GS-7 level may be appointed using the Outstanding Scholar provision if they possess at least a 3.5 GPA or have graduated in the upper ten percent of the class. Evaluation methods: Applicants will be evaluated on experience, education and training, awards, and supervisory appraisal. How to apply: Applicants may submit a resume, the Optional Form for Federal Employment (OF-612), or any other written format, including the SF-171. In addition, nonstatus applicants must submit a college transcript (the transcript must include grades through the summer 1997 semester). Status (federal) applicants must also submit a copy of their latest Notification of Personnel Action (SF-50) and copy of performance appraisal issued within the last 12 months to U.S. Department of Justice.

State University Paralegal

Job Summary: Assists attorneys with trial and pretrial matters. Job duties: Organizes, enters, and cross-references documents in a computerized database. Obtains, assembles, and organizes documents pertinent to litigation. Prepares discovery requests and responses. Assists in the preparation of statements and declarations of witnesses. Assists general counsel in organizing and carrying out special projects as assigned. Performs other related duties as assigned or requested. Job qualifications: Must have specialized paralegal training and one year of experience. May combine experience and education as substitute for minimum education or experience. Prefer a bachelor's degree, certificate from an ABA-approved program, and two years of experience. Skills: Must have the ability to assemble and coordinate manuscripts, compose letters, gather data, input data, communicate with others to gather information, maintain filing systems, prioritize different projects, research information, schedule appointments, write memorandums for own signature, coordinate work of others. Must operate personal computer, photocopier, and word processor.

City Attorney's Office/Internal Litigation Unit Paralegals

This is paraprofessional legal work of moderate difficulty assisting attorneys in case preparation and processing. An employee of this class is responsible for performing paraprofessional legal tasks routinely handled by attorneys and assisting in the coordination of case activities. Some positions may require working part time or evenings (until 9 P.M.) or require the ability to communicate in Spanish. Minimum qualifications: More than one year of experience in a private or governmental law firm performing primarily litigation related case management and legal research under the direction of an attorney; an associate degree or a certificate of completion from an accredited college or technical school as a legal assistant or paralegal; or an equivalent combination of education, experience, and training that provides the desired knowledge, skills, and abilities.

Nonprofit Organizations

Nonprofit organizations that hire paralegals may be advocacy groups, such as poverty law organizations that provide legal services to disadvantaged persons, or activist groups, such as environmental, women's, or civil rights groups. Often the same group will participate in both activities. For the most part, people who work for these organizations do so because they believe in the cause; the pay usually isn't good. The non-monetary rewards of these jobs are significant, however. Nonprofits, although they are serious about the work they do, can rarely be described as stuffy. Usually the office environment is quite casual, and the staff is open to new ideas.

Advocacy nonprofit organizations include groups such as Legal Services Corporation (LSC), a private corporation that was established by Congress in 1974 to provide equal access to the law for impoverished Americans. LSC offices have very limited budgets, as is true of most nonprofits. They occasionally hire paralegals, but they are perhaps better sources for volunteer internships. If you do decide to work for a nonprofit, you may find the work stressful at times, but when you are working for a cause you believe in, it's very rewarding.

As with corporate jobs, sometimes nonprofits aren't looking for a paralegal, but your training will nonetheless qualify you for the position they are trying to fill. If you are committed to working for a nonprofit group, keep your eyes open for all sorts of job titles.

Sample Job Advertisements

Immigration Paralegal

A national, public interest law firm dedicated to protecting and promoting the rights of low-income immigrants through impact litigation, policy analysis, training, technical assistance, and the publication of training materials is looking for a paralegal to add to our staff of 11. Qualifications: Prefer four-year college degree or paralegal training. At least two years of responsible paralegal experience in which independent judgment was utilized and client interaction was emphasized. Thorough knowledge of legal procedures. Familiarity with immigration law and a second language are a plus. Salary: $31,704.47 to $40,515.59.

Community Organizer

A community organization whose goals are to empower parents with the necessary skills to help their children succeed in school, to bring the community and delinquent youth together, and to help citizens take action to improve their neighborhoods needs a community organizer. Job duties include conducting constituent interviews, research, recruiting volunteers, developing volunteer leaders, implementing issue campaigns, writing, media relations, and fundraising. Hours: 45 to 50 hours per week (most evenings; occasional weekends); flextime. Qualifications: Four-year college degree, excellent written and oral communications skills, commitment to grassroots organizing and citizen empowerment; bilingual (Spanish) and computer skills are helpful. Salary: $21,000 to $24,000 (depending on experience); health insurance and two weeks vacation.

Planned Giving / Major Gifts Paralegal

International non-governmental human rights organization is seeking an assistant to the Advisor for Planned Giving. Responsibilities: Management of terminated estates, bequests, and trusts and administrative assistance to a multimillion-dollar fundraising program that seeks estate-related gifts throughout the United States. Qualifications: The selected candidate must have three years of paralegal or banking experience specifically related to estates/bequests/trusts. Successful candidates will have management experience in a legal estates department, or as a paralegal handling estates, or as a banker trained in managed trusts. Administration duties include word processing.

Other Workplaces

In addition to full-time jobs with the workplaces described above, paralegals may be employed for short-term projects by those same employers. The three types of short-term employment are contract, independent, and temporary. All have the advantage of flexibility and great variety in the tasks the paralegal is asked to perform. While most of this work is best suited for paralegals with some experience, there are some temporary agencies that place recent graduates.

Contract Paralegals

Contract, or freelance, paralegals are hired by attorneys or companies to work on a case-by-case basis. The benefits of self-employment include the freedom to structure your own time and to choose the projects you want to work on. The disadvantages include uncertainty about your income and the necessity of paying your own business expenses. In addition, you must be able to market yourself.

Independent Paralegals

Independent paralegals work directly with clients. Since their work is not supervised by an attorney, independent paralegals may not work in every state (see the section earlier in this chapter regarding the unauthorized practice of law); some states define paralegals, in part, as those who work under the supervision of a lawyer. Independent paralegals help consumers, for example, fill out forms for bankruptcy, estate planning, and taxes. However, they still cannot give legal advice. So your clients need to know before they come to you which bankruptcy chapter they should file under, for example, or whether they should set up a trust. Once these matters have been determined by the client in conjunction with a lawyer, however, the client can save money by hiring a paralegal rather than a lawyer to fill out the forms.

Independent paralegals should ideally have several years of experience. Because of the risk of being accused of practicing law without a license, you must be absolutely certain what is within your legal domain and what is not. As mentioned above, there are some states that won't allow independent paralegals to work as such at all.

Temporary Paralegals

Some paralegals prefer to work through temporary agencies. Some are placed by general temporary employment companies, such as the international franchises Kelly and Manpower. In larger cities, legal temporary agencies are sprouting up. These agencies place attorneys, paralegals, and legal secretaries in temporary positions. Many people enjoy temporary work; it gives you more control over your own time than full-time employment, with a bit more security than freelancing. If, as you finish your paralegal training, you're still unsure about the kind of paralegal work you'd like to specialize in, temporary placements give you an opportunity to try out a variety of positions, however it is less secure than full-time employment. You may have periods in which the agency has no assignment for you, and at times you may have to take positions that you aren't interested in.

DO YOU HAVE WHAT IT TAKES TO BE A PARALEGAL?

Successful paralegals possess certain skills. Some of the skills you may have already mastered, and some you will need to acquire. For each skill listed below, consider whether, at this time it is one you already have, one that needs some work, or one that you need to learn.

	highly skilled	needs work	need to learn
Communication skills	_____	_____	_____
Research skills	_____	_____	_____
Organization skills	_____	_____	_____
Prioritizing skills	_____	_____	_____
Independent thinking	_____	_____	_____
Analytical skills	_____	_____	_____
Investigative skills	_____	_____	_____
Concentration skills	_____	_____	_____
Computer skills	_____	_____	_____

Organization, prioritizing, independent thinking, and the ability to concentrate on several projects at the same time are vital to a successful paralegal. Legal research skills will be taught in paralegal programs, but if you feel that your general research skills are lacking, you may want to do some studying on your own. Consult the appendices at the end of this book for help. Analytical and investigative tasks that paralegals undertake are specialized to the law—and you will learn them in a good program.

The two most important areas in which a paralegal should excel are communications and computers. It is absolutely vital that you are able to communicate effectively, both orally and in writing. And in even the smallest, most rural law offices, computers are becoming more and more common, and dependence on computer research is growing every day. Most paralegal job offers indicate the software they expect you to be familiar with, and won't interview a candidate without computer proficiency.

Communication

In the legal field, you must be able to do more than make yourself understood. You must be able to express yourself accurately, succinctly, and correctly. Look back over the grades you received in English and any other classes in which you had to write or speak. Think back over comments you received about your work. If you need to, ask a teacher or school counselor for an assessment of your communication skills. If you feel they are lacking, it is imperative that you improve in this area. Be sure you choose a training program that offers courses in writing, and take them all. There are also writing courses offered online, and at community colleges.

Computer Skills

Most paralegal programs require, or at least make available, computer training. Keep in mind that there are two skills you need to master. One is the ability to use a computer and common business software; the other is the ability to perform legal research on a computer. Both of these are vitally important. If you run across a paralegal program that doesn't teach computer assisted legal research, don't attend. It won't adequately prepare you for a career as a legal assistant.

Depending on the amount of computer training you have already received in your years in school or at work, the ideal paralegal training course will 1) offer you the opportunity to learn/improve your basic keyboarding skills; 2) introduce you to commonly used computer software (legal-specific programs include Abacus Law, Summation Blaze, and TimeSlips); and 3) offer you training in WestLaw and LEXIS, computer legal research programs. WestLaw and LEXIS are subscription services; there are other research services on the Web, such as V. Law. A good computer research class will introduce you to several of these services and allow you the opportunity to practice using them.

Final Words

You have read about what makes a good paralegal, what paralegals do, and where they work. You have been provided with an overview of the job market, and how stiffer competition means that training and certification are becoming more important than ever. After you decide that this exciting career is for you, you will need to spend time and money getting trained. Chapter 2 explains everything you will need to know about the different types of programs, and schools that offer them. In Chapter 3, you will learn how to pay for your training. You are on your way to employment as a paralegal!

THE INSIDE TRACK

Who: Amanda Leff

What: Former Legal Assistant, Sullivan & Cromwell

                  Currently a graduate student in English at New York University

Where: New York City

INSIDER'S STORY

As an English major about to graduate from Yale, I felt that there weren't a lot of fields open to people like me. I didn't want to be a teacher, and after four years of college, I knew that I wanted to jump right into the work world. Becoming a paralegal seemed like a good option—with overtime, you can make as much as $50,000 your first year—enough to live in Manhattan. I was also toying with the idea of going to law school, so paralegal work would offer me a chance to test out the profession.

I found out about becoming a paralegal through undergraduate career services at college. Because I started my job search while I was still in school, I relied on on-campus recruiting: I submitted resumes through my college career services office to the law firms recruiting on campus, and had on-campus interviews; only after passing the first-round interviews did I interview at the firms themselves. I also asked around and found a few people working at big New York City firms that were not recruiting on campus. I contacted these people, asked them about their firms, and had them pass my resume on to human resources. I also talked to a few attorneys about being a paralegal and working at a corporate law firm. Although I didn't personally know any paralegals, I found that networking with lawyers gave me a pretty good idea of what the job would entail, which was especially helpful for my interviews.

From my brief stint as a paralegal, I learned a valuable lesson, and I strongly suggest that anyone considering law as a profession work for a year or two as a paralegal first—you will find out whether or not you're cut out for the profession. Many people go to law school these days simply for lack of anything better to do, and I think that's a big mistake; law—corporate law, in particular—often requires an aggressive, type-A personality. To be successful, you have to be willing to spend years working very long hours, having virtually no personal life, and doing pretty mundane work—and this is essentially what you'll do as a paralegal, too. Being a paralegal quickly convinced me that the legal profession was not for me. If you don't like being a legal assistant, it is likely that you won't like being a corporate lawyer.

On required skills: Everyone writes on their resume or cover letter that they have good "interpersonal skills," but you'll really, really need them to be a paralegal. You have to deal with a wide range of personalities—administrators, other paralegals, and the sometimes "dreaded" lawyers. Big law firms enforce a very strict hierarchy—the paralegals are the indentured servants of the associates, who are in turn the indentured servants of the partners. If you can't manage and smooth out difficult relationships, you'll have a hard time making it as a paralegal. It is also essential for a paralegal to have very good language skills: a lot of what you'll be doing is editing and proofreading briefs and other documents. Another major duty of a paralegal is research—in the library, on the Internet, and using services like LEXIS and WestLaw.

Ultimately, the most important characteristic that a paralegal should possess is a tendency to be obsessive compulsive. You will be managing huge quantities of documents, files, and information. You need to be fanatical about labeling things, color-coding things, and creating "systems" to organize things. You might be working on a case involving hundreds of thousands of pieces of paper, and you will be responsible for numbering every single sheet, making sure nothing gets lost, and being able to find the tiniest, most insignificant bit of information at a moment's notice. If you are a big-picture person, and can't be bothered with details, being a paralegal is not a good career fit for you.

Where you work as a paralegal is also important. Being a paralegal at a big law firm is totally different than being a paralegal at a small law firm. When you work at a big firm, you get all the perks that a big corporation can offer: you can expense cars and taxis home late at night, you get free dinners, corporate discounts on health clubs and theater tickets, and so on. You also get to work on some very high profile cases. However, you also get fewer responsibilities—big firms have armies of associates and they like their associates to write all of their own briefs. At a smaller firm, you would get to actually write legal documents, rather than just edit them. Small firms can also be a lot cozier. In an intimate working environment, you can really develop good professional relationships. On the other hand, if you don't like a particular person or situation at a small firm, it can make your daily routine difficult.

Another good reason to try your hand at paralegal work is that if you didn't get accepted at the law school of your choice, being a paralegal for a year or two can improve your odds of getting in. And, rumor has it that a firm will usually offer you a job after you graduate law school if you have worked there as a paralegal throughout law school.

For me, finding out what you don't want to do is as valuable as figuring out what you *do* want to do. I realized that the legal profession wasn't for me, and I switched careers. I'm now pursuing a Ph.D. in English Literature.

CHAPTER two

GETTING THE EDUCATION YOU NEED

NOW THAT you've decided on a career as a paralegal, you will need to take steps to prepare yourself to land your first job and enter the field. Those who hire paralegals agree that, in most markets, in order to get hired and succeed once you are on the job, you will need a college degree and/or a certificate. This chapter details the educational opportunities available, how to choose the one that's right for you, and how to get the most out of your program once you make your selection.

THE NATIONAL Federation of Paralegal Associations (NFPA) reports that over 85% of paralegals receive some sort of formal education. That's an enormous number, considering that less than forty years ago, when the profession began, there was only one way to receive paralegal training: on the job. Some paralegals began their careers as legal secretaries and gradually took on greater responsibility; others had bachelor's degrees and were hired as paralegal trainees.

The first paralegal school didn't appear until the late 1960s; by 1971, there were still less than a dozen. Today, aspiring legal assistants can choose from over 800 programs offered by community colleges, two- and four-year colleges and universities, business colleges, and proprietary institutions across the United States. Over 200 of those programs are approved by the American Bar Association.

Although the Bureau of Labor Statistics reports that the profession is among the fastest growing in the country, they also note that competition for paralegal positions is becoming stiffer. Why? One important reason is the large number of people obtaining paralegal education; the 800+ programs across the country turn out thousands of qualified paralegals each year. Those greater numbers mean that hiring firms can be more particular about employment offers.

But even with the tremendous growth of the paralegal field and the education of those working within it, there is still no national standard or licensing required of schools or their students. Unlike professions such as teaching and even plumbing, no state currently requires paralegals to be licensed and, as a result, no standardization of educational programs or criteria for employment has been established. The American Bar Association (ABA) and organizations such as the American Association for Paralegal Education (AAfPE) are attempting to change that. The ABA has been approving programs since 1975, and many employers look for paralegals who have attended these approved programs.

While in some areas of the country it is possible to get a job without formal training, most of those hired have a bachelor's degree. And even if you find an opportunity for on-the-job training, it can be a lonely and limiting way to receive your training. As Audrey Casey, a former paralegal, noted, "I wish I'd had that opportunity [to receive paralegal training] because it's much more isolated and difficult, doing it on your own." Surveys of law firms and corporate legal departments around the country confirm the fact that, in order to compete in today's job market, and land a job in your chosen career, you will need some kind of formal paralegal training. Outlined in this chapter are the various educational opportunities available.

According to the 1995 Compensation and Benefits Survey Conducted by the NFPA:

6% of paralegals have completed less than 30 semester hours of college

14% have at least 30 semester hours of college credits

20% have an associate degree

54% have a bachelor's degree

6% have a graduate degree, Ph.D., or J.D.

TYPES OF TRAINING PROGRAMS

While the following programs are remarkably similar, there are some key differences of which you should be aware when deciding what educational route to take. Later in this chapter, we'll discuss the selection process, showing you how to match your needs with the right program and the right school.

Certificate Programs

Many types of educational institutions offer paralegal certificate programs. Generally, you can expect business schools or other proprietary institutions to provide shorter courses that may require just a high school diploma for admission. These programs usually take about three months to complete 18 credits or semester units. Sometimes, these credits are transferable if you decide later to pursue a college degree.

Community colleges, and some two- and four-year colleges and universities offer another type of certificate program. It is geared toward those who already hold an associate or bachelor's degree. This program can take up to two years of full-time study to complete approximately 60 credits or semester units, and includes both general and paralegal-specific courses.

In a post-bachelor's certificate program, you can get the education you need to become a paralegal in a year or less, if you already possess a bachelor's degree. This type of program is offered at colleges and universities, and may bestow college credits, which can then be applied to an advanced degree. The following is a sample curriculum from a post-baccalaureate certificate program. It is approved by the American Bar Association, and is offered at Lansing Community College in Michigan. Total fees for a resident completing the program in one year are $1678.00; for an out-of-state student, they are $3592.00

One-year Paralegal Certificate Program Curriculum

Course	Credits
Ethics	3
Legal Research I	3
Legal Writing I	3
Litigation Procedures	4
Tort Law	2
Business Law I	3
Legal Research and Writing II	3
Commercial Law	3
Real Estate Transactions	3
Administrative Law	3
Legal Assistant Internship	3
Total credits	33

Source: www.lansing.cc.mi.us. If you are interested in learning about Lansing's program, log onto www.lcc.edu.careers/legal.

Associate Degree Programs

The associate degree is received after a student completes a two-year program (60–70 semester units) offered most commonly by community and two-year colleges. Approximately one-half of the program is made up of law courses, and the remainder are general education classes in fields of study such as English, math, science, and the humanities. Most students will have the opportunity to choose as many as two classes per semester; however, the majority of the curriculum is predetermined. The City College of San Francisco offers a two-year program in paralegal studies; upon completion, graduates receive the associate in arts degree, with an Award of Achievement in Legal Assistant/Paralegal. Here is the curriculum:

First Semester
Introduction to Legal Assisting
Introduction to Legal Writing
Commercial Law

    Legal Resources
    Human Relations
Second Semester
    Civil Litigation
    Commercial Law
    Legal Research and Writing
Third Semester
    Tort Law and Claims Investigation
    Wills, Trust, and Probate Administration
    Law-Office Management
Fourth Semester
    Family Law
    Legal Aspects of Evidence
    Investigation, Discovery, and Trial Preparation

Bachelor's Degree Programs

Four-year colleges and universities confer bachelor's degrees. A student is expected to complete about 120 semester hours of work; approximately 18 to 45 of those hours will be law-related, depending on whether the program is a major or a minor in paralegal studies. A bachelor's program usually combines general education, business, and legal courses. If you are just finishing high school, enrolling in a four-year liberal arts program allows you time to mature and provides skills that are necessary for the workplace. If you have an associate degree, your credits are often transferable to a four-year institution, bringing you much closer to the goal of obtaining a bachelor's degree.

The following is the curriculum for a bachelor's degree, from the Department of Government at Eastern Kentucky University, which offers a major in paralegal science. In addition to completing 76 hours of general requirements and electives, legal studies students take 40 hours in major requirements and twelve in supporting requirements, for a total of 128 semester hours. The program usually takes four years to complete, and costs $18,480.00 per year for an in-state student, including tuition, room and board, and books.

Major requirement course	Hours
LAS 210 Intro to Law	3
LAS 220 Legal Research and Writing I	3
LAS 300 Legal Research and Writing II	3
LAS 320 Civil Law and Liability	3
LAS 325 Real Estate/Bankruptcy Practice	3
LAS 350 Litigation Practice and Procedure	3
LAS 385 Legal Administration/ Computer Application	3
LAS 399 Paralegal Internship	4
LAS 410 Paralegal Seminar	3
Major electives (pick four)	
LAS 330 Family Law	3
LAS 340 Criminal Law Practice and Procedure	3
LAS 360 Probate Practice and Procedure	3
LAS 370 Corporation and Business Organization Practice	3
LAS 380 Administrative Agency Practice	3
LAS 460 Estate Planning and Procedure	3
LAS 490 Independent Study of Law	3
Supporting requirement courses	
ACC 201 Accounting	3
ENG 301 Advanced English Composition	3
POL 101 American Government	3
Supporting elective (pick one)	
POL 460 Law and Society	3
POL 463 Constitutional Politics	3
POL 464 Civil Liberties	3

Source: www.paralegal.eku.edu/

Master's Degree Programs

Master's degree programs are not the same as post-bachelor's certificate programs. Both, of course, require a bachelor's degree for admission, but a master's program may also require a graduate school admissions test, such as the GRE (Graduate Record Examination) or even the LSAT (Law School Admission Test). Upon completion of the program, you will be granted a master of arts or science degree (universities use different designations). Master's programs usually take a minimum of two years to complete and frequently require a thesis or similar project for graduation.

If you already have a bachelor's degree, obtaining a master's degree in paralegal studies may enhance your employability over those who have a bachelor's degree and earned a certificate instead. Because the phenomenal growth of the legal assistant field translates into more training programs that are graduating more paralegals, setting yourself apart from others may help you better compete for and land jobs. However, you should thoroughly investigate the market in which you will work before making a decision about an advanced degree; in some markets you may be considered "overeducated" when employers have the option of hiring paralegals with an associate degree or certificate instead.

One caveat about master's degree programs: they are not all intended to provide training to those working in the paralegal profession. Some are designed instead to give legal training to people who are already successful in another profession—in other words, people who believe their current position would be enhanced with legal training. Programs are usually quite clear about which type of student they were created for, so it is up to you to do the research and find the one best suited to your needs and career plans. For instance, Montclair State University in New Jersey, whose Master's in Legal Studies curriculum is detailed on the following page, notes that their graduates' career options include "advancement to supervisory and managerial positions in the legal environment; personnel, compliance and affirmative action officer positions in the private and public sectors; paralegal management and human resource officer positions; legal research and investigation work; private dispute resolution services; professional opportunities related to criminal justice and legal advocacy and education."

The curriculum of a master's program focuses exclusively on the subject in which you are obtaining a degree, so don't expect to find any of the "core" courses offered in an undergraduate curriculum. The Master of Arts degree in legal studies at Montclair State offers specialization in general legal studies, dispute resolution, or law office management and technology. Students must complete 36 credit hours of graduate-level courses. They also are required to complete a master's thesis on an approved topic. The degree costs approximately $8,500.00 per year for in-state residents, including tuition and fees.

Required courses for all students	Credit hours
LSLW501 Ethical and Professional Issues in the Legal Environment	3
LSLW511 Research Methods and Analysis	3
LSLW600 Thesis Seminar in Legal Studies	3
Department electives (choose nine)	
LSLW512 Statutory and Regulatory Analysis	3
LSLW520 Private Civil Responsibility: Contracts and Torts	3
LSLW531 Administrative Practice and Procedure	3
LSLW538 Trademark Law	3
LSLW540 Criminal Trial Preparation	3
LSLW541 Advanced Computer Systems in the Legal Environment	3
LSLW545 Cyber Law	3
LSLW550 Law Office Management and Technology	3
LSLW551 Negotiation Theory and Practice	3
LSLW552 Mediation Theory and Practice	3
LSLW553 Arbitration and Other Alternative Adjudicative Processes	3
LSLW554 Conflict Management/ Peer Mediation in Schools	3
LSLW555 Family Mediation	3
LSLW556 Dispute Resolution in the Workplace	3
LSLW557 Law Office Financial Management	3
LSLW558 Cross-Cultural Conflict Resolution	3
LSLW572 Legal Information Management	3
LSLW574 Human Rights Law	3
LSLW578 Legal Aspects of Human Resource Management	3
LSLW579 Private Sector Compliance with Public Regulations	3
LSLW580 Field Experience in Legal Studies	3
or	**Credit hours**
LSLW581 Cooperative Education in Legal Studies	3
LSLW599 Selected Topics in Legal Studies	3
LSPR411 Advanced Patent, Trademark, and Copyright	3
LSPR420 Advanced Civil Litigation	3
LSPR460 Advanced Legal Research and Writing	3

Source: www.chss.montclair.edu/leclair/LS/mals.html

Distance Education

Distance education—formerly referred to as *correspondence school*—is also an option for paralegal training. These programs differ from those offered at schools in that you are instructed through a variety of delivery systems, rather than the traditional teacher-and-students-in-the-classroom setup. Some rely heavily on the computer, providing Web-based interactive lessons over the Internet, while others allow you to read texts and take exams at your own pace. Increasingly, interactive video broadcasts to distant sites are being used. This involves your attendance in one location to watch an instructor giving a lesson from another. You have the opportunity to interact with your teacher and other students through the use of video cameras and monitors. The most attractive feature of distance learning is flexibility; for most of these programs, you can work in your home, at your own pace.

You need to be highly organized, disciplined, and motivated to succeed in distance education, and some people shy away from it for these same reasons. The National Institute for Paralegal Arts and Sciences notes, "The skills you learn to be successful as a distance education student are the exact skills you need to be an effective paralegal. Organization, self-reliance, motivation, the desire to learn, the will to succeed, and the ability to solve problems and make decisions are all a part of the distance education and paralegal processes. Success as a self-directed student demonstrates to your employer that you are goal-oriented and have the ability to work independently. Employer surveys taken over the last ten years have indicated overwhelming satisfaction with graduates of accredited paralegal distance education training programs."

If home study seems like the best option for you, use the criteria that follows when choosing a program. Then also consider the type of delivery system used, and determine not only your own familiarity with the technology (if any), but also whether the institution provides student training and technical assistance during the course. Find out how much interaction takes place among teachers and students during courses—are teachers available via phone, e-mail, or meeting in-person?

Ask the school for the names of former students whom you can contact for information about their experiences with the school. Get complete information on the course of study, and compare it with the curricula of schools you know to be reputable. Make sure that the distance education school you choose is accredited by an organization such as the Distance Education and Training Council (www.detc.org). The U.S. Department of Education can tell you about other accrediting agencies; contact them at 400 Maryland Avenue, SW, Washington, DC 20202-0498 (1-800-872-5327), or online at www.ed.gov. Finally, check with the Chamber of Commerce, the Better Business Bureau, or the attorney general's office in the state where the school is headquartered to see if the school has had complaints lodged against it.

The following is the curriculum for a certificate in Paralegal Sciences from the National Institute for Paralegal Arts and Sciences (NIPAS). The NIPAS is a correspondence school established in 1976; it provides distance education courses that result in a certificate or associate degree.

Course	Description
Introduction to Paralegal Studies:	Distance education learning plan, the paralegal profession, what paralegals do, how to transform yourself into a distance education student and begin your job search.
Criminal Law:	Detention, arrest, booking, probable cause, Constitutional protections, court and trial procedures, plea negotiations, element of crimes, Miranda warnings, indictments, investigation, legal research.
Business Organizations:	Corporations, sole proprietorships, partnerships, limited partnerships, formation, promotion, and management of each, Articles of Incorporation, by-laws, stock ownership, and government relations.
Wills, Trusts, and Estate Planning:	Will preparation, elements of a will, drafting, execution; the responsibilities of personal representatives; contesting, revoking, and terminating a will; classes of trusts; rules governing trusts; purposes of estate planning; probate; and guardianships.

Interviewing/Investigation/ The American Legal System:	Ethical aspects of interviewing and confidentiality; types of interviews, clients, and witnesses; how to prepare for an interview; questioning techniques, client psychology, qualities of a good investigator; finding the facts; locating witnesses; the U.S. Constitution; basis of American law.
Contracts:	Elements of contracts, different classifications and types of contracts, illegal contracts, unilateral contracts, bi-lateral contracts, breach of contract, promises, modifications, conditions, performance, and remedies.
Family Law:	Divorce, custody, and support, marriage contracts, antenuptial contracts, postnuptial and separation agreements, cohabitation, property settlements, and adoption.
Debtor/Creditor Relations and Bankruptcy:	Collection of debts, Fair Debt Collection Act, Federal Wage Garnishment Act, creditors' remedies, Chapter 7, Chapter 11, and Chapter 13 bankruptcy proceedings, alternatives to bankruptcy.
Billing/Bookkeeping/ Law Office Management:	Billable and non-billable hours, client billing, accounts receivable and payable, law firm bank accounts, the law office environment, management theory and functions, and personnel management.
Ethics:	Confidentiality, conflict of interest, the unauthorized practice of law, advertising and solicitation, zealous representation, client funds, and competence.
Legal Research:	Legal research is one of the most important duties that a paralegal performs. How to find and analyze the law and put this law into usable form is presented.
Civil Litigation/Torts/ Administrative Law:	Trial preparation, court systems, case management, service of process, pleadings, motions, stages of discovery, depositions and interrogatories, trial notebooks, settlement, the steps in a trial, post-trial procedures, torts, defenses, negligence, and personal injury.

Real Estate Law:	Ownership interests in real estate; easements, adverse possession, and real covenants; leases, condominiums, cooperatives, planned unit developments, Federal Government regulations; titles, mortgages, and deeds; alternatives to financing; and closings.
Preparation for the Paralegal Profession/ Comprehensive Examination:	This is a review of the legal subject matter covered in all previous lesson plans. The comprehensive final exam helps students prepare for other qualifying exams or job application tests they may take.

CHOOSING A PROGRAM

Selecting the paralegal training program that will best suit your needs, likes, and goals means making many decisions, including those about the type of school (community college, proprietary school, or two- or four-year institution), overall size of the school, location, and quality of programs. Would you prefer a single-sex or co-ed environment? Large classes held in lecture halls, or smaller classes in which you get to know your professors? Do you want to go a local school and live at home, or are you willing to relocate and perhaps live in on-campus housing?

You can explore these options and many others by enlisting the help of an experienced high-school guidance counselor or career counselor. Keep asking questions—of yourself and them—until you have the information you need to make your decision. If you are not currently in school, use the guidebooks listed in this chapter, and the resources listed in Appendix B to help you. And whether in school or not, you should talk with those who are already working in the legal field about their experiences. Ask where they went to school, what advantages they gained from their education, and what they would do differently if they were starting again.

Which Type of School Is Right for You?

As mentioned earlier in this chapter, there are five types of programs offered at four types of schools. From what you've already read, you probably have a good idea as to the program you're interested in, based on your current level of education and career goals. Check the boxes below to see which program(s) is (are) best suited to you. Then, read on to explore the types of schools that offer paralegal programs.

Degree you have:	High School or GED	Associate	Bachelor's
Programs you can attend:	Certificate_____	Certificate_____	Certificate_____
	Associate_____	Bachelor's_____	Master's_____

Usual Length of Program:

Certificate	Associate	Bachelor's*	Master's
Varies	two-year	four-year	two-year

*Bachelor's degrees in paralegal studies are relatively unusual, but that doesn't mean that you should discount the idea of getting a bachelor's degree. If the college you want to attend doesn't have a program, you may be able to design a bachelor's degree that will fit your needs. Many business and political science departments offer law courses; if the college is affiliated with a law school, undergraduates may be able to take some law courses. Talk to a counselor at the college or university you are interested in for more information.

If you are interested in a certificate program, will live at home, and work while getting your education, you might consider a community college or proprietary school. Community colleges are public institutions offering vocational and academic courses both during the day and at night. They typically cost less than two- and four-year public and private institutions. Proprietary schools are privately owned, but also tend to cost less than two- and four-year schools. Both community colleges and proprietary institutions usually require a high school diploma or GED for admission.

You can find out the location of Community Colleges in your area by contacting your state's Department of Higher Education (listed in Appendix B). Or check the World Wide Web through a search engine such as Yahoo.com for community colleges, which are listed by state. Proprietary schools may also be found on the Internet. Use the search term "paralegal education" to get started.

Just the Facts

Still in high school? You may be able to receive some college credits by enrolling as a "guest student" or auditor at your local community college. Get a copy of the school's course list, and pick out one or two you are interested in. Then, contact the admissions director. Explain your career plans and interest in sitting in on a course. You will have to pay for it, but in many cases the credit is transferable when you enter college for a degree.

Junior colleges are two-year institutions that are usually more expensive than community colleges because they tend to be privately owned. You can earn a two-year degree (AA or AS), which can usually be applied to four-year programs at most colleges and universities. Use the Internet or Peterson's *Two-Year Colleges* to help you with your search.

Colleges and universities offer undergraduate (usually four-year) programs in which you can earn a bachelor's (and often master's and doctoral) degree in a variety of fields. Entrance requirements are more stringent than for community colleges; admissions personnel will expect you to have taken certain classes in high school to meet their admission standards. Your high school GPA (grade point average) and standardized test scores (most often the SAT or ACT) will be considered. If your high school grades are weak or it has been some time since you were last in school, you might want to consider taking courses at a community college first. You can always apply to the college or university as a transfer student after your academic track record has improved.

Be aware that state or public colleges and universities are usually less expensive to attend than private colleges and universities because they receive state funds to offset their operational costs. Another thing to consider when choosing a college is whether they have placement programs for paralegals. Do they have a relationship with those in the area who hire paralegals, in which the employers actively recruit on campus? Attending a school with such a relationship could greatly improve your chances of employment upon graduation.

Online College Guides

Most of these sites offer similar information, including various search methods, the ability to apply to many schools online, financial aid and scholarship information, and online practice tests (PSAT, SAT, etc.). Some offer advice in selecting schools, give virtual campus tours, and help you decide what classes to take in high school. It is well worth it to visit several of them.

www.embark.com—a good general site

www.collegequest.com—run by Peterson's, a well-known publisher of college guide books (they can also be found at www.petersons.com)

www.review.com—a service of The Princeton Review. Plenty of "insider information" on schools, custom searches for schools, pointers on improving standardized test scores

www.collegenet.com—on the Web since 1995, best for applying to schools online

www.collegereview.com—offers good general information, plus virtual campus tours

www.theadmissionsoffice.com—answers your questions about the application process, how to improve your chances of getting accepted, when to take tests

EVALUATING YOUR NEEDS

You have now read about the types of training available, and the types of schools that offer this training. Before making a final decision, you will want to consider two more things: your needs and the quality of the schools you are interested in. First, make a determination about what you want and need from a paralegal training program in terms of:

Location
Finances
Scheduling

Read through the descriptions of these concerns below, and make notes regarding your position on each of them.

Where to Get Your Training

There are excellent paralegal training programs offered at schools throughout the country. To select one, you will need to decide where you want to be while getting your education. As mentioned earlier, it makes sense to attend a program located in the geographical area in which you want to work, for a number of reasons. Markets vary even within states, so it's important that you know as much as you can about the area you will be working in. For instance, law firms in small rural towns may have smaller budgets, and pay lower salaries than their big city counterparts just a few hundred miles away. Those smaller firms are more likely to hire certificate holders rather than paralegals with master's degrees. If you think you will work in one of those smaller markets, it wouldn't pay for you to get an advanced degree. In fact, you might be considered overeducated, and have a difficult time finding employment there.

Another advantage to attending school in the market in which you want to work is that you learn the laws of that area. Laws can vary a great deal from state to state, and instructors will most likely focus on those that pertain to their area. If you attend school far from where you will be job-hunting, you may not be as attractive a candidate as those who've already learned the local law. Finally, attending school where you will later work allows you to make contacts for future job hunting. Your school may help with job placement locally, and may also employ attorneys and others who hire paralegals. Your instructors can thus be later sources of employment. Networking is discussed in greater detail in Chapter 5, but keep in mind that having friends from school when you're out in the job market can be a big help.

However, if you can't attend a program in the place where you want to work, there are a number of things you can do to ensure future success. If you know where you are going to work after you complete your paralegal education, research that area to find out what kind of training most paralegals receive, and duplicate it as best you can. If you're not sure where you are going to end up, it's up to you to make the most of the education you do receive. Are you unable to attend an ABA-accredited school? Try to attend one that at least meets ABA standards. Also, rely on your internships and the faculty of the school you attend. Most of these people will be lawyers who may have attended law school in the market in which you plan to work. Well-trained legal assistants, with good references from their internships and professors, are always in demand.

College Guidebooks

Fiske, Edward B. *The Fiske Guide to Colleges 2002* (New York: Crown Publishing Group, 2001).
Fiske is the former education editor of the *New York Times*. His guide focuses on the "best and most interesting" 300+ colleges and universities. They are selected on the basis of their academic strength. Also included is a list of "best buys."

***Barron's Profiles of American Colleges* (New York: College Division of Barron's Educational Series, 2001).**

This book rates every accredited four-year college and university in the United States. It includes an index of majors, so you can zero in on those schools offering the program you want.

The Staff of the Yale *Daily News*. *The Insider's Guide to the Colleges* (New York: St. Martin's Press, 2000).

The most frank of the guides, and the only one researched and written by current college students. There are no statistics, course descriptions, or other "dry" information. What you will find is student-to-student advice on the admissions process, how to choose a school, and how to pay for your education, and portraits of the schools that cover many aspects of life on campus, including the condition of the dorms, and the dating scene.

***Peterson's Four Year Colleges, 2002* (Lawrenceville, NJ: Thomson, Peterson's Guides, 2001).**

This comprehensive bestseller covers all the basics.

Finances

Costs of the various programs, and the differences in costs between each type of school, have been touched on earlier in this chapter. Now, you will need to think more specifically about what you can afford. While there are many sources of funding for your education (check out Chapter 3), and schools do sometimes offer full or partial scholarships, you will still need to spend some money in order to get a quality paralegal training. When evaluating the schools you're interested in, be sure to find out all the costs, not just tuition. You will have to purchase books, which can cost hundreds of dollars over the course of the program (and over a thousand dollars if you're considering a bachelor's degree). If you live away from home, you will need to pay for room and board, which can total as much as your tuition at some schools. Will you need childcare while attending classes, or have to drive long distances to get to school? Consider those additional costs when calculating how much you will have to spend.

Don't rule out any schools in which you have an interest at this point. Just be sure to gather as much information as you can about real cost of attendance. Read through Chapter 3 to understand all of your options regarding financing your education. Then, you will be prepared to make an informed decision about which program to attend in terms of what you can afford.

Scheduling

When making a choice about paralegal training, you should also think about your schedule, and the commitments you may already have made. For instance, do you currently have a job you would like to continue working at while you're in school? You will need to find a program that offers classes at times when you're not working. Will an internship interfere with your employment? It might be a good idea to speak with your employer about your plans and goals. He or she may be willing to offer some flexibility.

If you have young children at home, or some other responsibility that requires your time, consider how you will manage both that responsibility and your education. Some schools offer low-cost childcare to their students. Or perhaps another family member or friend could help while you're attending classes or studying. Be sure to think through all of the potential obstacles to your training, and seek out ways to overcome them.

Another option is part-time attendance. The length of each type of training program listed on page 49 refers to full-time study, except for distance education, which is usually estimated to include a student's part-time job or family responsibilities. If you are under financial constraints, you can spread the cost of the program over a greater amount of time. If you have young children at home, need to continue working while getting your education, or have another time constraint, part-time attendance can allow you the flexibility your busy schedule demands. But be aware that while both the financial and time commitments to the program are significantly reduced, it is only for the short term. In total, you will have spent the same, or more, time and money getting your degree or certificate.

When you've considered what you want in terms of the type of program, location, costs, and scheduling, you will be able to make a decision about the type of school to attend. Now, you will need to evaluate those schools that meet your criteria in order to find the one that best suits your needs.

Evaluating the Schools

By now, you should be able to make decisions about the type of program and school you would like to attend, significantly narrowing down the number of schools that you are considering. After consulting the list of programs in Appendix C, as well as the other resources in this chapter, make a list of the school or schools offering what you want. You may be lucky enough to find the final decision quite easy; if not, here are some more things to keep in mind while evaluating the programs on your finalist list.

As mentioned above, there is no national standard for paralegal education, so it is somewhat difficult to compare programs academically. However, there are some national organizations that provide guidelines that may be helpful to you. For instance, the National Federation of Paralegal Associations, Inc. (NFPA) has come up with a list of courses they believe constitute a well-rounded curriculum. The NFPA states that legal assistant students "need to have exposure to the following theory/practice areas":

Litigation and Civil Procedure
Legal Research and Writing
Real Property Transactions
Business and Corporate Law
Wills, and Trust and Estate Planning
Family Law
Torts
Contracts

The NFPA also notes that other subjects may be desirable, depending on the market you will be working in, and any specialties you may be considering. Look for additional courses such as:

Advanced Legal Research and Writing
Advanced Litigation and Civil Procedure
Bankruptcy and Debtor/Creditor Rights
Administrative Law
Pension and Profit Sharing
Law Office Economics and Management

Tax Law
Labor Relations and Employment Law
Intellectual Property
Criminal Law
Immigration Law
Social Security Law
Constitutional Law
Environmental Law
Elder Law

In addition to legal courses, it's important that a program offer courses in paralegal ethics. Once you're on the job, the information you get from such a course will help guide you in maintaining your proper role in the legal field. Since only trained attorneys who have been admitted to the bar of a particular state can give legal advice, paralegals must do their job without giving such advice (which could constitute the unlicensed practice of law, a punishable offense). This is not always as clear as it may seem. As a paralegal, you may, for example, help someone fill out a bankruptcy form. You may not, however, help them decide which kind of bankruptcy to file; that constitutes giving legal advice. A separate paralegal ethics course is preferable; some schools, however, may choose to teach ethics throughout the curriculum, in conjunction with the other law classes.

Another place to look for guidance when evaluating programs is the American Association for Paralegal Education (AAfPE). Established in 1981, this organization's mission is to promote high educational standards for paralegals. In its Statement of Academic Quality, AAfPE asserts that paralegal training requires a curriculum that includes both substantive legal knowledge and practical skills. This rigorous course of study needs to give instruction in the areas that paralegals need as professionals. AAfPE recognizes seven essential components of a quality program: curriculum development, facilities, faculty, marketing and promotion, paralegal instruction, student services, and related competencies.

When you find a program or programs that interest you, the AAfPE recommends that you ask the questions listed below. If you don't have enough information, call the school's admissions director and either ask the questions directly or request more information in the form of school brochures, course descriptions, and other documents. Since many schools have their own websites, you may be able to find your answers on the Internet.

1. *What is the reputation of the institution and the paralegal program?*

   The general public and the legal community should hold the institution offering the program and the program itself in high regard. Check with people you know in the community, in the legal field, and in higher education for information.

2. *What services are offered to students?*

   Assistance should be offered in these areas: orientation, tutoring, academic counseling, financial aid, career information and counseling, and placement assistance. Information on the placement rate and job satisfaction of graduates should be available.

3. *What facilities are available to students?*

   Schools should have a legal research library, computer laboratories, and properly furnished classrooms. Facilities should accommodate students with disabilities.

4. *What activities are available to students?*

   Students should have the opportunity to participate in such activities as honor societies and volunteer work in the legal community. Information about paralegal associations and continuing paralegal education should be available.

5. *What is the mission of the institution and what are the goals of the paralegal program?*

   The mission and goals should be clearly stated in the institutional and program literature. You should assess whether the mission and goals match your individual needs.

6. *What is the content and nature of the curriculum?*

   The courses should teach practical job skills in conjunction with the underlying legal theory. The curriculum should cover legal research and writing, litigation, ethics, contracts, business organizations, and torts. Courses should develop students' critical thinking, communication, computational, computer, and organizational skills, and competency to handle ethical issues. Programs should offer an experiential learning component such as an internship, practicum, or clinical experience.

7. *What are the graduation requirements?*

   Students should be required to take both paralegal and general education courses unless students have completed general education prior to enrollment.

8. *What are the backgrounds of the program director and faculty?*

These professionals should have the appropriate academic credentials, such as a law degree or formal paralegal education; program directors may also have advanced degrees in related areas. Many have experience in the legal field. Faculty members should have expertise and experience in the subject areas they teach and experience working with or as paralegals. The program director and faculty must be committed to the role of the paralegal in the delivery of legal services.

Source: This list was excerpted from the brochure *How to Choose a Paralegal Program*, published jointly by the American Association for Paralegal Education, American Bar Association, Association of Legal Administrators, Legal Assistant Management Association, National Association of Legal Assistants, and the National Federation of Paralegal Associations; it can be found at www.aafpe.org/choose.html.

Accreditation by the American Bar Association is another standard by which you can measure the quality of training programs. The ABA has been approving paralegal education programs since 1975 based on its strict quality guidelines. They look at an institution's curriculum, faculty, administration, academic resources, student services, and library facilities. Because of a lack of national standards or requirements, the approval process is voluntary. When a program seeks ABA approval, it must be offered by an institution that is accredited by an accrediting agency on an approved list. If it meets this standard, the program seeking approval must submit a detailed self-evaluation report with supporting documents. The ABA then sends an evaluation team to visit the school. Approval is granted for a period of seven years. As of February 1999, the paralegal programs at 232 institutions across the country have been approved. A few new programs are usually approved each year.

Keep in mind, though, that there are many fine programs that choose not to seek ABA accreditation. But of those that don't, many schools still model their programs on the ABA guidelines, which can be useful in distinguishing one school from another. The best schools will follow the ABA guidelines fairly closely. In order to be considered for ABA accreditation, a legal assistant program must be a post-secondary school program that:

▶ is part of an accredited educational institution.
▶ offers at least 60 semester hours (or the equivalent) of classroom work, including general education classes and at least 18 semester hours of law courses.

▶ is advised by a committee comprised of attorneys and legal assistants from the public and private sectors.

▶ has qualified instructors who are committed to paralegal education.

▶ has student services available, including placement and counseling.

▶ has an adequate legal library available.

▶ has appropriate facilities and equipment.

Make sure that even if the program isn't accredited by the ABA, the school is accredited. There are a variety of accrediting agencies, depending on the kind of school in question. Examples include the Accrediting Council for Independent Colleges and Schools (ACICS), New England Schools and Colleges (NESC), and Distance Education and Training Council (DETC). In addition, in some states the program itself may be accredited or approved by the state bar association. The faculty should be comprised of people who are committed to paralegal education and who are up to date on changes in the legal assistant field. This may mean practicing attorneys, but it really isn't necessary for everyone on the faculty to be a practicing attorney. Practicing legal assistants, and former attorneys and paralegals who are dedicated to paralegal education, are perfectly fine instructors.

Try to get a feel for the available student services. These should include, at a minimum, counseling and placement. In a small school, the teaching staff may take most of the responsibility for these tasks. Just make sure that the staff seems as committed to those parts of their job as they are to teaching. A faculty comprised of only practicing attorneys and paralegals might be hard to find when you need one-on-one attention. Make sure they have regular office hours during which you can meet with them. Finally, make sure that the program you are interested in has access to a decent law library, such as one at a law school or courthouse.

ADVICE ON APPLYING TO A PARALEGAL PROGRAM

Kevin Huntington is the admissions officer at the Minnesota Paralegal Institute in Minnetonka, Minnesota. He offers these words on applying to paralegal programs:

Basically, the advice we give to people who are interested in applying to our program is to research the field and make sure it's something that they definitely want to do. We have a really low attrition rate, and one of the reasons is that we screen people before we allow them into the program, to make sure not only that they are going to be good for our program, but also that our program is going to be good for them.

We don't look for any specific background or any particular experience, provided the student has a good GPA and a bachelor's degree, and passes the entrance exam. If he or she passes those screening devices, our main concern is that after they graduate and get the certificate, our students will be able to find employment that's satisfactory to them—employment that they will enjoy. So before applying, be sure to research the field and know exactly what you're getting into. As long as it's something you want to do, we're happy to let you into our school. And help you get to where you want to be.

PROFESSIONAL CERTIFICATION

As mentioned in Chapter 1, there are currently two certifications available to qualified paralegals: Certified Legal Assistant (CLA), administered by the National Association of Legal Assistants (NALA), and the Paralegal Advanced Competency Exam (PACE), administered by the National Federation of Paralegal Associations, Inc. (NFPA). Please note that these are not the same kinds of certificates as those you receive when you complete a certificate programs; those indicate that you have completed a course of education. The CLA and PACE are professional designations that refer to one or more of the following: education, experience, and successful testing. If you are interested in obtaining one or both of these certifications, keep in mind the requirements you will have to meet when choosing your training program.

The CLA is a credentialing program that was established by the National Association of Legal Assistants in 1976. In order to sit for the CLA (take their test), a paralegal must meet one of the following requirements:

1. Graduation from a paralegal training program that is accredited by the American Bar Association; or a program that is authorized to award an associate degree; or a post-bachelor's certificate program in legal assistant studies; or a bachelor's degree program in paralegal studies; or a legal assistant program that consists of a minimum of 60 semester hours (or the equivalent), of which at least 15 semester hours are substantive legal courses
2. A bachelor's degree in any field and one year of experience as a legal assistant (successful completion of at least 15 semester hours of substantive legal courses will be considered equivalent to one year's experience as a legal assistant)
3. A high school diploma or GED and seven years experience as a legal assistant under the supervision of a member of the bar, plus a minimum of twenty hours of continuing legal education credit, completed within a two-year period prior to the examination date

Specifics of the examination are discussed in Chapter 1.

In order to sit for the PACE, a legal assistant must meet all of the following requirements:

1. At least two years of paralegal experience
2. A bachelor's degree
3. Completion of a paralegal program at an accredited school (paralegal education need not be separate from the bachelor's degree; until December 31, 2000, paralegals who were lacking a bachelor's degree or completion of a paralegal program could substitute four years of paralegal experience)
4. No felony convictions or revoked license, registration, or certification

Details of this examination are also discussed in Chapter 1.

Although it is possible to take the CLA test as soon as you graduate from a paralegal program, most legal assistants wait until they have a few years of experience before obtaining a certification. It's not a bad idea to keep the standards in mind, though.

Note: When you are job-hunting, keep in mind the difference between having a certificate (because you graduated from a paralegal program) and having certification (either CLA or PACE). Employers may be confused about this, and when they advertise for a "certified" paralegal, they may actually mean a legal assistant with a certificate conferred after completion of a training program.

STATE CERTIFICATION

There are currently three states that provide special paralegal certification programs. California, Florida, and Louisiana are at the forefront of the movement toward a national standard for paralegal education.

California Advanced Specialization Certification for Paralegals

Established in 1995, the California Advanced Specialist (CAS) Certification was created for California paralegals who have achieved the national CLA (Certified Legal Assistant) credential and want to demonstrate advanced knowledge of California law and procedure. To qualify for the California Advanced Examination, these legal assistants have successfully completed a two-day examination covering general skills and knowledge required of legal assistants, and have demonstrated proficiency in a specialty practice area. Specialty certification in California is available in the areas of Civil Litigation, Business Organizations/Business Law, Real Estate, Estates and Trusts, and Family Law. As of December 1999, there were 30 legal assistants in California who achieved the CAS credential. For further details about the program, contact NALA Headquarters or the Commission for Advanced California Paralegal Specialization, Inc., P.O. Box 22433, Santa Barbara, California 93121.

Florida Certification Program

Established in 1980, the Florida Legal Assistant Inc.'s certification program (the CFLA) complements the NALA's CLA program. Its purpose is to provide a standard for measurement of advanced skills and knowledge in Florida law of those persons who have already achieved the national CLA certification.

FLA, Inc.™ began administering the CFLA exam in 1983. As NALA's largest affiliate association in the State of Florida, FLA, Inc. ™, was the first in the nation to administer such an exam for the state level. There are presently 121 CFLAs in the State of Florida.

The CFLA examination is administered through the Certifying Board of FLA, Inc.™ in conjunction with the FLA, Inc.™ mid-year meeting in the spring and the annual meeting in September. The exam takes three hours and is limited to Florida law. A two-day CFLA review course has also been established. FLA, Inc.™, has developed a CFLA study guide, which is available from FLA, Inc.™ Headquarters at a cost of $75 plus shipping.

Upon successful completion of the CFLA examination, a legal assistant becomes authorized to use the designation "CFLA" with the "CLA" or "CLAS" designation. CFLAs are required to have 30 hours of continuing legal education credit over a five-year period to maintain their CFLA certification, which must be directly applicable to Florida law. Proof of continuing legal education must be submitted to and is maintained by the Certifying Board.

For further information, call:

FLORIDA LEGAL ASSISTANT, INC. HEADQUARTERS
www.flainc.org
Tel: 800-433-4352
Certifying Board Chair—Rosemary F. Wheeler, CLA, CFLA
E-mail: RoWheeler3@aol.com

Louisiana Certified Paralegal Program

October 4–5, 1996—First Testing Session
At its 1992 annual meeting, the members of the Louisiana State Paralegal Association (LSPA) passed a resolution that endorsed voluntary certification as a means of establishing professional standards and promoting recognition of the paralegal profession. Subsequently, LSPA determined that a state voluntary certification credential should be developed and made available to all Louisiana paralegals who desire to demonstrate a comprehensive knowledge, a high degree of proficiency in Louisiana Law, and adherence to a Code of Ethics to enhance the quality of paralegal services available to the Louisiana legal community and to the public it serves.

The resulting certification program requires the candidate to sit for both the LCP (Louisiana Certified Paralegal) and CLA (Certified Legal Assistant) examinations. The LCP examination is designed to test the examinee's knowledge and understanding of Louisiana legal and judicial system, Louisiana general law, ethics, civil procedure, and four areas of Louisiana substantive law. The CLA examination offered by the National Association of Legal Assistants tests the core paralegal skills, knowledge of the American legal and judicial system, and four areas of substantive law based on Federal law and common law principles. To qualify for the examination, one must either have a valid CLA credential or meet one of the alternate eligibility requirements of the CLA examination. The examination is offered twice a year, in October and in the spring (March or April). Applications are due six weeks prior to the examination date.

As a state specific examination, the LCP examination is designed to test a paralegal's knowledge and comprehension of the law in the State of Louisiana. Each examinee will be required to take the General Law, Ethics, and Civil Procedures sections and must select four law topics, from a list of eight, that will comprise the substantive law section of that examinee's test. The substantive law areas are:

Business Organizations
Contracts/Obligations
Criminal Law and Procedure
Wills/Probate/Successions/Trusts
Family Law
Property
Torts
Evidence

There are two ways to prepare for the examination. In order to study or learn Louisiana law as it pertains to the paralegal, it is suggested that prospective examinees consult a current textbook covering the topics selected for the substantive law section. Much of the material covered in this section of the examination is acquired through experience in the legal field. LSPA offers a review course once a year to assist interested parties in preparing for the examination. The written materials and a videotape of the seminar sessions are available from the Louisiana State Paralegal Association. For further information, contact:

NALA Headquarters
1516 South Boston, #200
Tulsa, OK 74119
Tel: 918-587-6828

Source: NALA; Copyright 2001, all rights reserved.

MAKING THE MOST OF YOUR TRAINING PROGRAM

Once you've chosen a program of study, completed the application process, and have then been accepted to that program, there are a number of ways to guarantee that the time, effort, and money you spend on the program are maximized.

Internships

An internship is one way to get job experience before you enter the "real" workforce. Many training programs include internships as part of their curriculum. Although there are basically three types, all internships are designed as learning experiences, giving the intern exposure to an actual working environment. Internships can be one of the following:

paid—the intern receives a salary for his/her work.
college—the intern is a student, and usually receives college credit for his/her work
summer—the intern is likely to be a student, who may or may not receive college credit

Opportunities for paralegal internships may be found in law offices, government agencies, corporate legal departments, and courthouses. College internships may be the easiest to find, because your school will place you, or help place you, in one. They have relationships with the offices and agencies that use interns, and place students with these companies year after year.

The companies that offer internships may also look to hire students when they complete their courses of study. For a college internship, you may also have to attend a class with other interns, prepare a journal detailing your work experience, or write a paper about it.

If your school does not provide help in finding internships, or does not offer credit for them, you can find one for yourself. There are a number of ways in which you can uncover an opportunity, either during the summer, a semester off, or once you have graduated. If your school hires lawyers to teach some courses, consider enrolling in them. You may be able to make a contact or contacts that could lead to an internship. The Internet is also a good source of information. There, you can learn about all stages of the internship experience, including identifying learning objectives, finding the "right office," managing "office politics," self-monitoring and documentation, and how to use the internship to land a permanent job. Three sites that offer listings of internships available nationwide are www.internships.com, www.internjobs.com, and www.vault.com.

The following books are also excellent resources:

Anselmi, John, et al. *The Yale Daily News Guide to Internships 2000* (NY: Kaplan, 1999).

Green, Marianne Erlich. *Internship Success: Real-World, Step-by-Step Advice on Getting the Most Out of Internships* (New York: McGraw-Hill, 1998).

Oldman, Mark, and Samer Hamadeh. *The Internship Bible 2001* (Princeton, NJ: Princeton Review, 2000).

Peterson's Guides, ed. *Peterson's Internships, 2002* (Princeton, NJ: Peterson's Guides, 2001).

When you locate specific internship opportunities, some of the questions you will want to ask include:

▶ How many work hours are required to receive credit?
▶ If applicable, how much does the internship pay?
▶ Will you be graded for your work? If so, by a college professor or the person you work under at the company you intern for?
▶ Do you have to arrange your own internship with the company or work through your school?
▶ Does the internship program at your school also require you to attend

classes, write a paper, or make a presentation to a faculty member in order to receive credit?

▶ What will your responsibilities be on a day-to-day basis?

▶ Who, within the company, will you be working for?

▶ Will the internship provide real world work experience that's directly related to your chosen field?

▶ Will your participation in the internship provide you with networking opportunities?

Once you land an internship, consider it an audition for ultimately obtaining a full-time job. Always act professionally, ask questions, follow directions, display plenty of enthusiasm, volunteer to take on additional responsibilities, meet deadlines, and work closely with your boss/supervisor. Upon graduating, make sure to highlight your internship work on your resume.

Having an internship on your resume will make you stand out to a recruiter for a number of reasons:

1. You are already familiar with a professional environment and know what is expected of you.
2. You have proven yourself through performance to a potential employer.
3. After evaluating the realities of the job, you are still eager to pursue it.

For all of the reasons detailed above, it makes great sense for you to get an internship. Claire Andrews, director of paralegal programs at Casco Bay College in Portland, Maine notes, "it's really important to me that the students do get out there, whether it's through a part-time job or through the internship, to get the practical experience. Otherwise, waving that certificate means nothing."

Getting the Most Out of Your Classes

The law is a discipline in which concepts build on one another. For this reason, the law lends itself well to an outline style of note-taking. For example, a student's notes from an evidence or trial practice course lecture on admitting evidence at trial might look like this:

I. Admitting Evidence
    A. Only if Relevant—if it tends to make a fact more or less likely than without it
    1. FRE 401—all rel. ev. admitted
    2. All rel. ev. must be:
        a. Probative—relationship between ev. and fact
        b. Material—link between fact and sub. law
    3. May be excluded if prob. value is outweighed by danger of:
        a. unfair prejudice—HOW DECIDE??
        b. confusion of issues
        c. misleading jury
        d. delay, waste of time or needless (because cumulative)
    B. Direct v. circumstantial ev.

If you haven't had much experience with outline formats, the table of contents of a textbook can be an effective starting point. Notice above how the use of abbreviations can make note-taking go faster. Students in this course have already been introduced to the Federal Rules of Evidence, which is abbreviated FRE (line I.A.1.). Also, this student has developed a habit of abbreviating repeated concepts rather than writing them out each time. So the word *relevant* becomes "rel." and the word *evidence* becomes "ev." "Sub. Law" (line I.A.2.b.) is *substantive law*, a concept that repeats in several classes. Some of these abbreviations you will come up with on your own; some have become pretty standard in the law.

Common Legal Abbreviations

K = contract

Δ = defendant

Π = plaintiff

v. = *versus*, as in *Brown v. Board of Education* (lawyers usually say the letter "v" rather than the word "versus")

e.g. = for example

i.e. = that is

∴ = therefore

FRE = Federal Rules of Evidence (a compilation of laws and cases, as is the following abbreviation)

CFR = Code of Federal Regulations

Notice that this student also made a note to find out more about I.A.3.a., *unfair prejudice*. This concept was not clearly presented in class, and the note serves as a reminder to investigate further.

The use of highlighters when reading class assignments can also help to organize information. You might decide to use different colors for the plaintiff, the defendant, the judge, state law versus federal law, and the new rules versus the old. Remember, the reason you are taking notes is to give yourself a concise and clear summary of each class session. Whatever method makes it most clear for you is a good method.

Because learning the law involves building concepts one on another, it is important to attend class regularly. It is also vital to be prepared, but if for some reason you are unable to prepare, don't use that as an excuse not to attend class. You need to do both, but one is better than neither. Each instructor conducts class differently, but to the extent that it is appropriate, participate in class. It is also helpful to briefly read over your notes as soon after class as possible to make sure you understand everything you've written.

Preparing for Exams

Begin preparing for an exam by reading over your notes. Look for any areas that you indicated you didn't understand at the time, and make sure you understand them now. If you don't, talk to your instructor or do some extra reading until the concept is clear. Then, try making an outline of the class. If you've taken good notes all along, you will simply put each day's notes in order. But if your notes are less that perfect, create an outline to study from. As an example, check out one of the commercial study aids for law school students, such as *Emanuel Law Outlines*, *Smith's Review*, or the *Black Letter Series*.

Most important, on the evening before the exam, relax, eat a good dinner, and get a good night's sleep. In the morning, eat a good breakfast (and lunch, if it's an afternoon test). Try to take a walk or get some other light exercise, if you have time before the exam. During the exam, stay calm and have faith in yourself and your abilities.

Your Social Life

During your training program, there will be interesting people sitting next to you in class and teaching your classes. These people have experiences and knowledge that can benefit you. You can help each other by studying together and creating an information "loop" that keeps everyone informed not only about what is happening in class, but throughout the school as well. Forging friendships with teachers and students can make the transition from student to paralegal easier as well. After graduation, these are the people who may be able to help you get your first job. They may also be your colleagues throughout your career.

If the program you're in offers social events, take advantage of them as often as you can. And make it a point early in your academic career to get to know those in your counseling and placement offices. These people know the answers to almost all your questions, and can be an invaluable resource.

Your paralegal education is the first essential step on the road to your chosen career. Don't view it simply as something to get through, as an ordeal you must overcome before you can begin work and start your real life. School is the time to learn as much about the profession and yourself as you possibly can. Along the way, you will make friends and contacts—sometimes they'll be the same person—who will be equally valuable to you as you finish school and embark on your career as a paralegal.

THE INSIDE TRACK

Who: Christy Lawrence

What: Legal Assistant

White Collar Crime and Litigation Sections

Akin, Gump, Strauss, Hauer, & Feld, LLP

Where: Dallas, Texas

INSIDER'S STORY

I began my career working as a legal secretary for a family law attorney in Texas. I then went to work for a larger firm, where I learned the importance of being a team player and about the many aspects of the law. After thirteen years as a legal secretary, I wanted to become more involved in the cases so I attended a paralegal certification program and received my paralegal certificate (*summa cum laude*). Because my secretarial position involved a lot of paralegal work, I already had an in-depth knowledge of research and litigation.

Soon after earning my certificate, I was promoted to paralegal. I became an active member of the Dallas Area Paralegal Association and made many contacts in the field. Joining a local paralegal association like this is a must for any new paralegal—it's a great way to network and learn from others. I also encourage paralegals to become involved with volunteering for local State Bar section activities.

My paralegal specialty is litigation. I was inspired to begin my own niche after viewing an edition of *Legal Assistant Today* that profiled four paralegals that created their own niche. I then began work to form a paralegal animal law section, since I have been involved in pro bono animal law on my own time. I have a strong desire to work for the protection of animals. I have since formed, and chair, the Dallas Area Paralegal Association's Animal Law Section (the first paralegal specialty section of its type in Texas). I was also appointed to serve as Chair of the Legal Assistants Committee within the State Bar of Texas Animal Law Section.

My most notable achievement is an article I wrote that was published in the Fall 2000 edition of the *National Paralegal Reporter*, "Maggie's Story." The article briefly described the animal cruelty statute in Texas, and also how paralegals could become involved in animal law. As a result of this article, I received numerous calls from paralegals in different states wanting assistance in forming an animal law section in their local paralegal organization. To date, two paralegals that I have assisted went on to form animal law sections within their local organizations (in New York and Pennsylvania). I am also working to form a paralegal animal law network, so that when animal law cases arise in different states, I will be able to furnish the assigned attorney with paralegal assistance in that state.

I cannot tell you how good it feels to be able to educate and assist other paralegals that are interested in animal law. I have earned the respect of local attorneys for educating practitioners as well as the public about this specific area of law. My goal is to complete my undergraduate work and attend law school, preferably one with an animal law curriculum.

I have encountered many great opportunities in the paralegal field, and I find it to be a very rewarding career, especially when you work on projects that you are truly committed to. Being involved in pro bono cases, and realizing that you were part of a team that actually made a difference in a person's or animal's life makes it all worthwhile. The work can be tough, but it is a great payoff to see something that you have worked on so hard come to fruition.

CHAPTER three

FINANCING YOUR EDUCATION

POST-SECONDARY education of any kind and duration can be quite expensive. However, that's no reason not to go to school; if you are determined to get training, there's financial aid available for you. This chapter explains the three types of financial aid available: scholarships and grants, loans, and work-study programs. You will find out how to determine your eligibility, which financial records you will need to gather, and how to complete and file forms (a sample financial aid form is included). At the end of the chapter are listed many more resources that can help you find the aid you need.

YOU HAVE decided on a career as a paralegal, and you have chosen a training program. Now, you need a plan for financing your training. Perhaps you or your family have been saving for your education, and you've got the money to pay your way. However, if you're like most students, you don't have enough to cover the cost of the training program you'd like to attend. Be assured that it is likely you can qualify for financial aid, even if you plan to attend school only part-time.

Because there are many types of financial aid, and the millions of dollars given away or loaned are available through so many sources, the process of finding funding for your education can seem confusing. Read through this chapter carefully, and check out the many resources, including websites and publications, listed in Appendix B. You will have a better understanding of where to look for financial aid, what you can qualify for, and how and when to apply.

Also take advantage of the financial aid office of the school you've chosen, or your guidance counselor if you're still in high school. These professionals can also offer plenty of information, and can help to guide you through the process. If you're not in school, and haven't chosen a program yet, look to the Internet. It's probably the best source for up-to-the-minute information, and almost all of it is free. There are a number of great sites at which you can fill out questionnaires with information about yourself, and receive lists of scholarships and other forms of financial aid for which you may qualify. You can also apply for some types of federal and state aid online.

SOME MYTHS ABOUT FINANCIAL AID

The subject of financial aid is often misunderstood. Here are three of the most common myths:

Myth #1. All the red tape involved in finding sources and applying for financial aid is too confusing for me.
Fact: It's really not that confusing. The whole financial aid process is a set of steps that are ordered and logical. Besides, several sources of help are available. To start, read this chapter carefully to get a helpful overview of the entire process and tips on how to get the most financial aid. Then, use one or more of the resources listed within this chapter and in the appendices for additional help. If you believe you will be able to cope with college, you will be able to cope with looking for the money to finance your education, especially if you take the process one step at a time in an organized manner.

Myth #2: For most students, financial aid just means getting a loan and going into heavy debt, which isn't worth it, or working while in school, which will lead to burnout and poor grades.
Fact: Both the federal government and individual schools award grants and scholarships, which the student doesn't have to pay back. It is also possible to get a combination of scholarships and loans. It's worth taking out a loan if it means attending the school you really want to attend, rather than settling for

your second choice or not going to school at all. As for working while in school, it's true that it is a challenge to hold down a full-time or even part-time job while in school. However, a small amount of work-study employment (10–12 hours per week) has been shown to actually improve academic performance, because it teaches students important time-management skills.

Myth #3. I can't understand the financial aid process because of all the unfamiliar terms and strange acronyms that are used.
Fact: While you will encounter an amazing number of acronyms and some unfamiliar terms while applying for federal financial aid, you can refer to the acronym list and glossary at the end of this chapter for quick definitions and clear explanations of the most commonly used terms and acronyms.

TYPES OF FINANCIAL AID

There are three categories of financial aid:

1. Grants and scholarships—aid that you don't have to pay back
2. Work-Study—aid that you earn by working
3. Loans—aid that you have to pay back

Each of these types of financial aid will be examined in greater detail, so you will be able to determine which one(s) to apply for, and when and how to apply. Note that the first two types of aid are available on four levels: federal, state, school, and private.

Grants

Grants are normally awarded based on financial need. Even if you believe you won't be eligible based on your own or your family's income, don't skip this section. There are some grants awarded for academic performance and other criteria. The two most common grants, the Pell Grant and Federal Supplemental Educational Opportunity Grant (SEOG), are both offered by the federal government.

Federal Pell Grants

Federal Pell Grants are based on financial need and are awarded only to undergraduate students who have not yet earned a bachelor's or professional degree. For many students, Pell Grants provide a foundation of financial aid to which other aid may be added. For the year 1999–2000, the maximum award was $3,125.00. You can receive only one Pell Grant in an award year, and you may not receive Pell Grant funds for more than one school at a time.

How much you get will depend not only on your Expected Family Contribution (EFC) but also on your cost of attendance, whether you're a full-time or part-time student, and whether you attend school for a full academic year or less. You can qualify for a Pell Grant even if you are only enrolled part time in a training program. You should also be aware that some private and school-based sources of financial aid will not consider your eligibility if you haven't first applied for a Pell Grant.

Federal Supplemental Educational Opportunity Grants (FSEOG)

FSEOGs are for undergraduates with exceptional financial need—that is, students with the lowest Expected Family Contributions (EFCs). They give priority to students who receive Pell Grants. An FSEOG is similar to a Pell Grant in that it doesn't need to be paid back.

You can receive between $100 and $4,000 a year, depending on when you apply, your level of need, and the funding level of the school you're attending. There's no guarantee that every eligible student will be able to receive an FSEOG. Students at each school are paid based on the availability of funds at that school and not all schools participate in this program. To have the best chances of getting this grant, apply as early as you can after January 1 of the year in which you plan to attend school.

State Grants

State grants are generally specific to the state in which you or your parents reside. If you and your parents live in the state in which you will attend school, you've got only one place to check. However, if you will attend school in another state, or your parents live in another state, be sure to check to see if you might be eligible. There is a list of state agencies in Appendix A, including telephone numbers and websites, so you can easily find out if there is a grant for which you can apply.

Scholarships

Scholarships are almost always awarded for academic merit or for special characteristics (for example, ethnic heritage, personal interests, sports, parents' career, college major, geographic location) rather than financial need. As with grants, you do not pay your award money back. Scholarships may be offered from federal, state, school, and private sources.

The best way to find scholarship money is to use one of the free search tools available on the Internet. After entering the appropriate information about yourself, a search takes place which ends with a list of those prizes for which you are eligible. Try www.fastasp.org, which bills itself as the world's largest and oldest private sector scholarship database. www.college-scholarships.com and www.gripvision.com are also good sites for conducting searches. If you don't have easy access to the Internet, or want to expand your search, your high school guidance counselors or college financial aid officers also have plenty of information about available scholarship money. Also, check out your local library.

To find private sources of aid, spend a few hours in the library looking at scholarship and fellowship books or consider a reasonably priced (under $30) scholarship search service. See the Resources section at the end of this chapter to find contact information for search services and scholarship book titles. Also contact some or all of the professional associations for paralegals; some offer scholarships, while others offer information about where to find scholarships. If you're currently employed, find out if your employer has aid funds available. If you're a dependent student, ask your parents and other relatives to check with groups or organizations they belong to for possible aid sources. Consider these popular sources of scholarship money:

religious organizations
fraternal organizations
clubs, such as the Rotary, Kiwanis, American Legion, or 4H
athletic clubs
veterans groups
ethnic group associations
unions

If you already know which school you will attend, check with a financial aid administrator (FAA) in the financial aid department to find out if you qualify for any school-based scholarships or other aid. Many schools offer merit-based aid for students with a high school GPA of a certain level or with a certain level of SAT scores in order to attract more students to their school. Check with the paralegal program's academic department to see if they maintain a bulletin board or other method of posting available scholarships.

While you are looking for sources of scholarships, continue to enhance your chances of winning one by participating in extracurricular events and volunteer activities. You should also obtain references from people who know you well and are leaders in the community, so you can submit their names and/or letters with your scholarship applications. Make a list of any awards you've received in the past or other honors that you could list on your scholarship application.

Scholarships

There are thousands of scholarships awarded to students planning to enter the paralegal profession. Below are a few samples. To find more sources, search the Internet with terms such as "paralegal and scholarship."

Career Advancement Scholarship

Offered by the Business and Professional Women's Foundation
2012 Massachusetts Avenue, NW
Washington, DC 20036
Number of awards: 100
Amount of award(s): $500–$1,000

Minimum age to apply: 25

For use by juniors or seniors attending any four-year college or university.

Applications accepted from current college sophomores and juniors.

Non-traditional students are encouraged to apply.

2002 Paralegal Scholarships

The National Federation of Paralegal Associations, Inc., in conjunction with West Publishing Group, is pleased to award two scholarships totaling $5,000. Scholarships of $3,500 and $1,500 will be presented at the 2002 NFPA Spring Convention in Indianapolis, Indiana May 2–5, 2002. West will provide a travel stipend for the two award recipients so that they may receive their awards at the NFPA Spring Convention.

Applicants must be part-time or full-time enrolled students or accepted students in a paralegal education program or college level program with emphasis in paralegal studies. They must demonstrate they have maintained a "B" average.

Selection will be based upon scholastic excellence, participation in campus and paralegal program leadership activities, community service, and review of the writing sample. Proven need for financial assistance *may* be considered. NFPA membership is not a requirement.

The National Honor Society in Paralegal/Legal Assistant Studies

Association for Paralegal Education (AAfPE) Scholarship

To be considered, please submit:

- AAfPE LEX SCHOLARSHIP Application
- 500-word typed essay stating your conclusions and reasoned opinions regarding the topic in the article printed on our website.
- The AAfPE LEX Scholarship Certification form
- An official transcript, which will demonstrate at least a B average
- A letter of recommendation from a faculty member

NOTE: The scholarship is to be used to continue the pursuit of the student's paralegal education. The AAfPE check will be made payable to the awardee and the awardee's school.

A program benefiting mainly middle-class students is the Hope Scholarship Credit. Eligible taxpayers may claim a credit for tuition and fees up to a maximum of $1,500.00 per student (the amount is scheduled to be re-indexed for inflation after 2001). The credit applies only to the first two years of post-secondary education, and students must be enrolled at least half-time. Families whose adjusted gross income is $80,000.00 or more are ineligible. To find out more about the Hope Scholarship credit, log onto www.sfas.com.

The National Merit Scholarship Corporation offers about 5,000 students scholarship money each year based solely on academic performance in high school. If you are a high school senior with excellent grades and high scores on tests such as the ACT or SAT, ask your guidance counselor for details about this scholarship.

You may also be eligible to receive a scholarship from your state (again, generally the state you reside in) or school. Check with the higher education department of the relevant state or states, or the financial aid office of the school you will attend.

Work-Study Programs

When applying to a college or university, you can indicate that you are interested in a work-study program. Their employment office will have information about how to earn money while getting your education. Work options include the following:

on- or off-campus
part-time or almost full-time
school- or nationally based
in the legal field (to gain experience) or not (just to pay the bills)
for money to repay student loans or to go directly toward educational expenses

If you're interested in school-based employment, you will be given the details about the types of jobs offered (they can range from giving tours of the campus to prospective students, to working in the cafeteria, or helping other students in the Financial Aid office) and how much they pay.

You may also want to investigate the Federal Work-Study (FWS) program, which can be applied for on the Free Application for Federal Student Aid (FAFSA). The FWS program provides jobs for undergraduate and graduate students with financial need, allowing them to earn money to help pay education expenses. It encourages community service work and provides hands-on experience related to your course of study, when available. The amount of the FWS award depends on:

when you apply (apply early!)
your level of need
the funds available at your particular school

Work-study salaries are the current federal minimum wage or higher, depending on the type of work and skills required. As an undergraduate, you will be paid by the hour (a graduate student may receive a salary), and you will receive the money directly from your school; you cannot be paid by commission or fee. The awards are not transferable from year to year, and you will need to check with the schools to which you're applying: not all schools have work-study programs in every area of study.

An advantage of working under the FWS program is that your earnings are exempt from FICA taxes if you are enrolled full-time and are working less than half-time. You will be assigned a job on-campus, in a private non-profit organization, or a public agency that offers a public service. Some schools have agreements with private for-profit companies, as long as those jobs are judged relevant to your course of study. The total hourly wages you earn in each year cannot exceed your total FWS award for that year and you cannot work more than twenty hours per week. Your financial aid administrator (FAA) or the direct employer must consider your class schedule and your academic progress before assigning your job.

For more information about National Work Study programs, visit the Corporation for National Service website (www.cns.gov) and/or contact:

▶ **National Civilian Community Corps (NCCC)**—This AmeriCorps program is an 11-month residential national service program intended for 18–24-year-olds. Participants receive $4,725.00 for college tuition or to help repay education loan debt. Contact:
   National Civilian Community Corps
   1100 Vermont Avenue, NW
   Washington, DC 20525
   Tel: 800-94-ACORPS.

▶ **Volunteers in Service to America (VISTA)**—VISTA is a part of ACTION, the deferral domestic volunteer agency. This program offers numerous benefits to college graduates with outstanding student loans. Contact:

VISTA
Washington, DC 20525
Tel: 800-424-8867

Student Loans

Although scholarships, grants, and work-study programs can help to offset the costs of higher education, they usually don't give you enough money to entirely pay your way. Most students who can't afford to pay for their entire education rely at least in part on student loans. The largest single source of these loans is the federal government. However, you can also find loan money from your state, school, and/or private sources.

Try these three sites for information about the United States government's programs:

www.fedmoney.org
This site explains everything from the application process (you can actually download the applications you will need), eligibility requirements and the different types of loans available.

www.finaid.org
Here, you can find a calculator for figuring out how much money your education will cost (and how much you will need to borrow), get instructions for filling out the necessary forms, and even information on the various types of military aid (which will be detailed in the next chapter).

www.ed.gov/offices/OSFAP/students
The Federal Student Financial Aid Homepage. The FAFSA (Free Application for Federal Student Aid) can be filled out and submitted online. You can find a sample FAFSA in Appendix D, to help familiarize yourself with its format.

You can also get excellent detailed information about different sources of federal education funding by sending away for a copy of the U.S. Department of Education's publication, *The Student Guide*. Write to:

Federal Student Aid Information Center
P.O. Box 84
Washington, DC 20044
Tel: 800-4FED-AID

Listed below are some of the most popular federal loan programs:

Federal Perkins Loans

A Perkins Loan has the lowest interest (currently, it's 5%) of any loan available for both undergraduate and graduate students, and is offered to students with exceptional financial need. You repay your school, which lends the money to you with government funds.

Depending on when you apply, your financial need, and the amount the school is given by the federal government, you can borrow up to $4,000 for each year of undergraduate study. The total amount you can borrow as an undergraduate is $20,000. If you are a graduate/professional student, you can borrow up to $6,000 per year and $40,000 total including undergraduate Perkins Loans.

The school pays you directly by check or credits your tuition account. You have a nine-month grace period after you graduate (provided you were continuously enrolled at least half-time) before you must begin repayment, with up to ten years to pay off the entire loan.

PLUS Loans (Parent Loans for Undergraduate Students)

PLUS Loans enable parents with good credit histories to borrow money to pay education expenses of a child who is a dependent undergraduate student enrolled at least half-time. Your parents must submit the completed forms to your school.

To be eligible, your parents will be required to pass a credit check. If they don't pass, they might still be able to receive a loan if they can show that extenuating circumstances exist or if someone who is able to pass the credit check agrees to co-sign the loan. Your parents must also meet citizenship requirements.

The yearly limit on a PLUS Loan is equal to your cost of attendance minus any other financial aid you receive. For instance, if your cost of attendance is $10,000 and you receive $8,000 in other financial aid, your parents could borrow up to, but no more than, $2,000. The interest rate varies, but cannot exceed 9% over the life of the loan. Your parents must begin repayment while you're still in school. There is no grace period.

Direct or FFEL Stafford Loans

Stafford Loans are low-interest loans that are given to students who attend school at least half-time. The lender is the U.S. Department of Education for the Direct Stafford Loan and a participating lender for the FFEL Stafford Loan. Stafford Loans fall into one of two categories:

▶ *Subsidized loans* are awarded on the basis of financial need. You will not be charged any interest before you begin repayment or during authorized periods of deferment. The federal government "subsidizes" the interest during these periods.
▶ *Unsubsidized loans* are not awarded on the basis of financial need. You will be charged interest from the time the loan is disbursed until it is paid in full. If you allow the interest to accumulate, it will be capitalized—that is, the interest will be added to the principal amount of your loan, and additional interest will be based upon the higher amount. This will increase the amount you have to repay.

There are many borrowing limit categories to these loans, depending on whether you get an unsubsidized or subsidized loan, which year in school you're enrolled, how long your program of study is, and if you're considered independent or dependent by the federal government. You can have both kinds of Stafford Loans at the same time, but the total amount of money loaned at any given time cannot exceed $23,000. The interest rate varies, but should not exceed 8.25% for new loans. An origination fee for a Stafford

Loan is approximately 3% or 4% of the loan, and the fee will be deducted from each loan disbursement you receive. There is a six-month grace period after graduation before you must start repaying the loan.

State Loans

Loan money is also available from state governments. In Appendix A you will find a list of the agencies responsible for giving out such loans, with websites and e-mail addresses when available. Remember that you may be able to qualify for a state loan based on your residency, your parents' residency, or the location of the school you're attending.

Questions to Ask Before You Take Out a Loan

In order to get the facts regarding the loan you're about to take out, ask the following questions:

1. What is the interest rate and how often is the interest capitalized? Your college's financial aid administrator (FAA) should be able to tell you this.

2. What fees will be charged? Government loans generally have an origination fee that goes to the federal government to help offset its costs, and a guarantee fee, which goes to a guaranty agency for insuring the loan. Both are deducted from the amount given to you.

3. Will I have to make any payments while still in school? Usually you won't, and, depending on the type of loan, the government may even pay the interest for you while you're in school.

4. What is the grace period—the period after my schooling ends—during which no payment is required? Is the grace period long enough, realistically, for you to find a job and get on your feet? (A six-month grace period is common.)

5. When will my first payment be due and approximately how much will it be? You can get a good preview of the repayment process from the answer to this question.

6. Who exactly will hold my loan? To whom will I be sending payments? Who should I contact with questions or inform of changes in my situation? Your loan may be sold by the original lender to a secondary market institution, in which case you will be notified as to the contact information for your new lender.

7. Will I have the right to pre-pay the loan, without penalty, at any time? Some loan programs allow pre-payment with no penalty but others do not.

8. Will deferments and forbearances be possible if I am temporarily unable to make payments? You need to find out how to apply for a deferment or forbearance if you need it.

9. Will the loan be canceled ("forgiven") if I become totally and permanently disabled, or if I die? This is always a good option to have on any loan you take out.

APPLYING FOR FINANCIAL AID

Now that you're aware of the types and sources of aid available, you will want to begin applying as soon as possible. You've heard about the Free Application for Federal Student Aid (FAFSA) many times in this chapter already, and have an idea of its importance. This is the form used by federal and state governments, as well as school and private funding sources, to determine your eligibility for grants, scholarships, and loans. The easiest way to get a copy is to log onto www.ed.gov/offices/OSFAP/students, where you can find help in completing the FAFSA, and then submit the form electronically when you are finished. You can also get a copy by calling 1-800-4-FED-AID, or stopping by your public library or your school's financial aid office. Be sure to get an original form, because photocopies of federal forms are not accepted.

The second step of the process is to create a financial aid calendar. Using any standard calendar, write in all of the application deadlines for each step of the financial aid process. This way all vital information will be in one location, so you can see at a glance what needs to be done when. Start this calendar by writing in the date you requested your FAFSA. Then mark down when you received it and when you sent in the completed form. Add important dates and deadlines for any other applications you need to complete for school-based or private aid as you progress though the financial aid process. Using and maintaining a calendar will help the whole financial aid process run more smoothly and give you peace of mind that the important dates are not forgotten.

When to Apply

Apply for financial aid as soon as possible after January 1 of the year in which you want to enroll in school. For example, if you want to begin school in the fall of 2002, then you should apply for financial aid as soon as possible after January 1, 2002. It is easier to complete the FAFSA after you have completed your tax return, so you may want to consider filing your taxes as early as possible as well. Do not sign, date, or send your application before January 1 of the year for which you are seeking aid. If you apply by mail, send your completed application in the envelope that came with the original application. The envelope is already addressed, and using it will make sure your application reaches the correct address. You cannot send it via FedEx or other overnight delivery service; the address does not accept overnight deliveries.

Many students lose out on thousands of dollars in grants and loans because they file too late. A financial aid administrator from New Jersey says:

> When you fill out the Free Application for Federal Student Aid (FAFSA), you are applying for all aid available, both federal and state, work-study, student loans, etc. The important thing is complying with the deadline date. Those students who do are considered for the Pell Grant, the FSEOG (Federal Supplemental Educational Opportunity Grant) and the Perkins Loan, which is the best loan as far as interest goes. Lots of students miss the June 30th deadline, and it can mean losing $2,480 from TAG (Tuition Assistance Grant), about $350 from WPCNJ, and another $1,100 from EOF (Equal Opportunity Fund). Students, usually the ones who need the money most, often ignore the deadlines.

After you mail in your completed FAFSA, your application will be processed in approximately four weeks. Then, you will receive a Student Aid Report (SAR) in the mail. The SAR will disclose your Expected Family Contribution (EFC), the number used to determine your eligibility for federal student aid. Each school you list on the application may also receive your application information if the school is set up to receive it electronically.

You must reapply for financial aid every year. However, after your first year, you will receive a SAR in the mail before the application deadline. If no corrections need to be made, you can just sign it and send it in.

Getting Your Forms Filed

Follow these three simple steps if you are not completing and submitting the FAFSA online:

1. Get an original FAFSA. Remember to pick up an original copy of this form, as photocopies are not acceptable.

2. Fill out the entire FAFSA as completely as possible. Make an appointment with a financial aid counselor if you need help. Read the forms completely, and don't skip any relevant portions.

3. Return the FAFSA before the deadline date. Financial aid counselors warn that many students don't file the forms before the deadline and lose out on available aid. Don't be one of those students!

Financial Need

Financial aid from many of the programs discussed in this chapter is awarded on the basis of need (the exceptions include unsubsidized Stafford, PLUS, and Consolidation loans, and some scholarships and grants). When you apply for federal student aid by completing the FAFSA, the information you report is used in a formula established by the U.S. Congress. The formula determines your Expected Family Contribution (EFC), an amount you and your family are expected to contribute toward your education. If your EFC is below a certain amount, you will be eligible for a Pell Grant, assuming you meet all other eligibility requirements.

There is no maximum EFC that defines eligibility for the other financial aid options. Instead, your EFC is used in an equation to determine your financial needs.

Cost of Attendance – EFC = Financial Need

A financial aid administrator calculates your cost of attendance and subtracts the amount you and your family are expected to contribute toward that cost. If there's anything left over, you're considered to have financial need.

Are You Considered Dependent or Independent?

Federal policy uses strict and specific criteria to make this designation, and that criteria applies to all applicants for federal student aid equally. A dependent student is expected to have parental contribution to school expenses, and an independent student is not. The parental contribution depends on the number of parents with earned income, their income and assets, the age of the older parent, the family size, and the number of family members enrolled in post-secondary education. Income is not just the adjusted gross income from the tax return, but also includes nontaxable income such as Social Security benefits and child support.

You're an independent student if at least one of the following applies to you:

▶ you were born before January 1, 1978
▶ you're married (even if you're separated)
▶ you have legal dependents other than a spouse who get more than half of their support from you and will continue to get that support during the award year
▶ you're an orphan or ward of the court (or were a ward of the court until age 18)
▶ you're a graduate or professional student
▶ you're a veteran of the U.S. Armed Forces—formerly engaged in active service in the U.S. Army, Navy, Air Force, Marines, or Coast Guard or as a cadet or midshipman at one of the service academies—released under a condition other than dishonorable. (ROTC students, members of the National Guard, and most reservists are not considered veterans, nor are cadets and midshipmen still enrolled in one of the military service academies.)

If you live with your parents and if they claimed you as a dependent on their last tax return then your need will be based on your parents' income. You do not qualify for independent status just because your parents have decided to not claim you as an exemption on their tax return (this used to be the case but is no longer) or do not want to provide financial support for your college education.

Students are classified as *dependent* or *independent* because federal student aid programs are based on the idea that students (and their parents or spouse, if applicable) have the primary responsibility for paying for their post-secondary, i.e., after high school, education.

Gathering Financial Records

Your financial need for most grants and loans depends on your financial situation. Now that you've determined if you are considered a dependent or independent student, you will know whose financial records you need to gather for this step of the process. If you are a dependent student, then you must gather not only your own financial records, but also those of your parents because you must report their income and assets as well as your own when you complete the FAFSA. If you are an independent student, then you need to gather only your own financial records (and those of your spouse if you're married). Gather your tax records from the year prior to the one in which you are applying. For example, if you apply for the fall of 2002, you will use your tax records from 2001.

To help you fill out the FAFSA, gather the following documents:

- U.S. Income Tax Returns (IRS Form 1040, 1040A, or 1040EZ) for the year that just ended and W-2 and 1099 forms
- Records of untaxed income, such as Social Security benefits, AFDC or ADC, child support, welfare, pensions, military subsistence allowances, and veterans' benefits
- Current bank statements and mortgage information
- Medical and dental expenses for the past year that weren't covered by health insurance
- Business and/or farm records
- Records of investments such as stocks, bonds, and mutual funds, as well as bank Certificates of Deposit (CDs) and recent statements from money market accounts
- Social Security number(s)

Even if you do not complete your federal income tax return until March or April, you should not wait to file your FAFSA until your tax returns are filed with the IRS. Instead, use estimated income information and submit the FAFSA, as noted earlier, just as soon as possible after January 1. Be as accurate as possible, knowing that you can correct estimates later.

Maximizing Your Eligibility for Loans and Scholarships

Loans and scholarships are often awarded based on an individual's eligibility. Depending on the type of loan or scholarship you pursue, the eligibility requirements will be different. EStudentLoan.com (**www.estudentloan.com/ workshop.asp**) offers the following tips and strategies for improving your eligibility when applying for loans and/or scholarships:

1. Save money in the parent's name, not the student's name.
2. Pay off consumer debt, such as credit card and auto loan balances.
3. Parents considering going back to school should do so at the same time as their children. The more family members in school simultaneously, the more aid may be available to each.
4. Spend student assets and income first, before other assets and income.
5. If you believe that your family's financial circumstances are unusual, make an appointment with the financial aid administrator at your school to review your case. Sometimes the school will be able to adjust your financial aid package to compensate.
6. Minimize capital gains.
7. Do not withdraw money from your retirement fund to pay for school. If you must use this money, borrow from your retirement fund.
8. Minimize educational debt.
9. Ask grandparents to wait until the grandchild graduates before giving them money to help with their education.
10. Trust funds are generally ineffective at sheltering money from the need analysis process, and can backfire on you.
11. If you have a second home, and you need a home equity loan, take the equity loan on the second home and pay off the mortgage on the primary home.

GENERAL GUIDELINES FOR LOANS

Before you commit yourself to any loans, be sure to keep in mind that they need to be repaid. Estimate realistically how much you will earn when you leave school, remembering that you will have other monthly obligations such as housing, food, and transportation expenses.

Once You're in School

Once you have your loan (or loans) and you're attending classes, don't forget about the responsibility of your loan. Keep a file of information on your loan that includes copies of all your loan documents and related correspondence, along with a record of all your payments. Open and read all your mail about your education loan.

Remember also that you are obligated by law to notify both your Financial Aid Administrator (FAA) and the holder or servicer of your loan if there is a change in your:

▶ name
▶ address
▶ enrollment status (dropping to less than half-time means that you will have to begin payment six months later)
▶ anticipated graduation date

After You Leave School

After graduation, you must begin repaying your student loan immediately, or begin after a grace period. For example, if you have a Stafford Loan you will be provided with a six-month grace period before your first payment is due; other types of loans have grace periods as well. If you haven't been out in the world of work before, with your loan repayment you will begin your credit history. If you make payments on time, you will build up a good credit rating, and credit will be easier for you to obtain for other things. Get off to a good start, so you don't run the risk of going into default. If you default (or refuse to pay back your loan) any number of the following things could happen to you as a result:

▶ have trouble getting any kind of credit in the future
▶ no longer qualify for federal or state educational financial aid
▶ have holds placed on your college records
▶ have your wages garnished
▶ have future federal income tax refunds taken
▶ have your assets seized

To avoid the negative consequences of going into default in your loan, be sure to do the following:

▶ Open and read all mail you receive about your education loans immediately.
▶ Make scheduled payments on time; since interest is calculated daily, delays can be costly.
▶ Contact your servicer immediately if you can't make payments on time; he or she may be able to get you into a graduated or income-sensitive/income contingent repayment plan or work with you to arrange a deferment or forbearance.

There are a few circumstances under which you won't have to repay your loan. If you become permanently and totally disabled, you probably will not have to (providing the disability did not exist prior to your obtaining the aid). Likewise if you die, if your school closes permanently in the middle of the term, or if you are erroneously certified for aid by the financial aid office, you generally are released from your loan obligation. However, if you're simply disappointed in your program of study or don't get the job you wanted after graduation, you are not relieved of your obligation.

Loan Repayment

When it comes time to repay your loan, you will make payments to your original lender, to a secondary market institution to which your lender has sold your loan, or to a loan servicing specialist acting as its agent to collect payments. At the beginning of the process, try to choose the lender who offers you the best benefits (for example, a lender who lets you pay electronically, offers lower interest rates to those who consistently pay on time, or who has a toll-free number to call 24 hours a day, seven days a week). Ask the financial aid administrator at your college to direct you to such lenders.

Be sure to check out your repayment options before borrowing. Lenders are required to offer repayment plans that will make it easier to pay back your loans. Your repayment options may include:

▶ *Standard repayment*: full principal and interest payments due each month throughout your loan term. You will pay the least amount of interest using the standard repayment plan, but your monthly payments may seem high when you're just out of school.

▶ *Graduated repayment*: interest-only or partial interest monthly payments due early in repayment. Payment amounts increase thereafter. Some lenders offer interest-only or partial interest repayment options, which provide the lowest initial monthly payments available.

▶ *Income-based repayment*: monthly payments are based on a percentage of your monthly income.

▶ *Consolidation loan*: allows the borrower to consolidate several types of federal student loans with various repayment schedules into one loan. This loan is designed to help student or parent borrowers simplify their loan repayments. The interest rate on a consolidation loan may be lower than what you're currently paying on one or more of your loans. The phone number for loan consolidation at the William D. Ford Direct Loan Program is 1-800-557-7392. Financial administrators recommend that you do not consolidate a Perkins Loan with any other loans since the interest on a Perkins Loan is already the lowest available. Loan consolidation is not available from all lenders.

▶ *Prepayment*: paying more than is required on your loan each month or in a lump sum is allowed for all federally sponsored loans at any time during the life of the loan without penalty. Prepayment will reduce the total cost of your loan.

It's quite possible—in fact likely—that while you're still in school your Federal Family Education Loan Program (FFELP) loan will be sold to a secondary market institution such as Sallie Mae. You will be notified of the sale by letter, and you need not worry if this happens—your loan terms and conditions will remain exactly the same or they may even improve. Indeed, the sale may give you repayment options and benefits that you would not have had otherwise. Your payments after you finish school and your requests for information should be directed to the new loan holder.

If you receive any interest-bearing student loans, you will have to attend exit counseling after graduation, where the loan lenders will tell you the total amount of debt and work out a payment schedule with you to determine the amount and dates of repayment. Many loans do not become due until at least six to nine months after you graduate, giving you a grace period. For example, you do not have to begin paying on the Perkins Loan until nine months after you graduate. This grace period is to give you time to find a good job and start earning money. However, during this time, you may have to pay the interest on your loan.

If for some reason you remain unemployed when your payments become due, you may receive an unemployment deferment for a certain length of time. For many loans, you will have a maximum repayment period of 10 years (excluding periods of deferment and forbearance).

THE MOST FREQUENTLY ASKED QUESTIONS ABOUT FINANCIAL AID

Here are answers to the most frequently asked questions about student financial aid:

1. *I probably don't qualify for aid—should I apply for it anyway?*
   Yes. Many students and families mistakenly think they don't qualify for aid and fail to apply. Remember that there are some sources of aid that are not based on need. The FAFSA form is free—there's no good reason for not applying.

2. *Do I need to be admitted at a particular university before I can apply for financial aid?*

   No. You can apply for financial aid any time after January 1 of the year you will be in school. However, to get the funds, you must be admitted and enrolled in school.

3. *Do I have to reapply for financial aid every year?*

   Yes, and if your financial circumstances change, you may get either more or less aid. After your first year you will receive a "Renewal Application" which contains preprinted information from the previous year's FAFSA. Renewal of your aid also depends on your making satisfactory progress toward a degree and achieving a minimum GPA.

4. *Are my parents responsible for my educational loans?*

   No. You and you alone are responsible, unless they endorse or co-sign your loan. Parents are, however, responsible for the federal PLUS Loans. If your parents (or grandparents or uncle or distant cousins) want to help pay off your loan, you can have your billing statements sent to their address.

5. *If I take a leave of absence from school, do I have to start repaying my loans?*

   Not immediately, but you will after the grace period. Generally, though, if you use your grace period up during your leave, you will have to begin repayment immediately after graduation, unless you apply for an extension of the grace period before it's used up.

6. *If I get assistance from another source, should I report it to the student financial aid office?*

   Yes—and, unfortunately, it's possible that your aid amount will be lowered accordingly. But you will get into trouble later on if you don't report it.

7. *Are federal work-study earnings taxable?*

   Yes, you must pay federal and state income tax, although you may be exempt from FICA taxes if you are enrolled full time and work less than 20 hours a week.

8. *My parents are separated or divorced. Which parent is responsible for filling out the FAFSA?*

   If your parents are separated or divorced, the custodial parent is responsible for filling out the FAFSA. The custodial parent is the parent with whom you lived with the most during the past 12 months.

Note that this is not necessarily the same as the parent who has legal custody. The question of which parent must fill out the FAFSA becomes complicated in many situations, so you should take your particular circumstance to the student financial aid office for help.

Financial Aid Checklist

_____ Explore your options as soon as possible once you've decided to begin a training program.

_____ Find out what your school requires and what financial aid they offer.

_____ Complete and mail the FAFSA as soon as possible after January.

_____ Complete and mail other applications by the deadlines.

_____ Gather loan application information and forms from your college financial aid office.

_____ Forward the signed loan application to your financial aid office. Don't forget to sign it.

_____ Carefully read all letters and notices from the school, the federal student aid processor, the need analysis service, and private scholarship organizations. Note whether financial aid will be sent before or after you are notified about admission, and how exactly you will receive the money.

_____ Return any requested documentation promptly to your financial aid office.

_____ Report any changes in your financial resources or expenses to your financial aid office so they can adjust your award accordingly.

_____ Re-apply each year.

Financial Aid Acronyms Key

COA	Cost of Attendance
CWS	College Work-Study
EFC	Expected Family Contribution
EFT	Electronic Funds Transfer
ESAR	Electronic Student Aid Report
ETS	Educational Testing Service
FAA	Financial Aid Administrator
FAF	Financial Aid Form
FAFSA	Free Application for Federal Student Aid
FAO	Financial Aid Office/Officer
FDSLP	Federal Direct Student Loan Program
FFELP	Federal Family Education Loan Program
FSEOG	Federal Supplemental Educational Opportunity Grant

FWS	Federal Work-Study
PC	Parent Contribution
PLUS	Parent Loan for Undergraduate Students
SAP	Satisfactory Academic Progress
SC	Student Contribution
USED	U.S. Department of Education

FINANCIAL AID TERMS—CLEARLY DEFINED

Accrued interest—Interest that accumulates on the unpaid principal balance of your loan.

Capitalization of interest—Addition of accrued interest to the principal balance of your loan that increases both your total debt and monthly payments.

Disbursement—Loan funds issued by the lender.

Grace period—Specified period of time after you graduate or leave school during which you need not make payments.

Deferment—A period when a borrower, who meets certain criteria, may suspend loan payments.

Forbearance—Temporary adjustment to repayment schedule for cases of financial hardship.

Default (you won't need this one, right?)—Failure to repay your education loan.

Delinquency (you won't need this one, either!)—Failure to make payments when due.

Holder—The institution that currently owns your loan.

In-school grace, and **deferment interest subsidy**—Interest the federal government pays for borrowers on some loans while the borrower is in school, during authorized deferments, and during grace periods.

Interest-only payment—A payment that covers only interest owed on the loan and none of the principal balance.

Interest—Cost you pay to borrow money.

Lender (Originator)—Puts up the money when you take out a loan. Most lenders are financial institutions, but some state agencies and schools make loans too.

Origination fee—Fee, deducted from the principal, which is paid to the federal government to offset its cost of the subsidy to borrowers under certain loan programs.

Principal—Amount you borrow, which may increase as a result of capitalization of interest, and the amount on which you pay interest.

Promissory note: Contract between you and the lender that includes all the terms and conditions under which you promise to repay your loan.

Secondary markets—Institutions that buy student loans from originating lenders, thus providing lenders with funds to make new loans.

Servicer—Organization that administers and collects your loan. May be either the holder of your loan or an agent acting on behalf of the holder.

Subsidized Stafford Loans—Loans based on financial need. The government pays the interest on a subsidized Stafford Loan for borrowers while they are in school and during specified deferment periods.

Unsubsidized Stafford Loans—Loans available to borrowers, regardless of family income. Unsubsidized Stafford Loan borrowers are responsible for the interest during in-school, deferment periods, and repayment.

FINANCIAL AID RESOURCES

In addition to the sources listed throughout this chapter, these are additional resources that may be used to obtain more information about financial aid.

Telephone Numbers

Federal Student Aid Information Center	800-4-FED-AID
(U.S. Department of Education) Hotline	(800-433-3243)
TDD Number for Hearing-Impaired	800-730-8913
For suspicion of fraud or abuse of	800-MIS-USED
federal aid	(800-647-8733)
Selective Service	847-688-6888
Immigration and Naturalization (INS)	415-705-4205
Internal Revenue Service (IRS)	800-829-1040
Social Security Administration	800-772-1213

National Merit Scholarship Corporation	708-866-5100
Sallie Mae's College AnswerSM Service	800-222-7183
Career College Association	202-336-6828
ACT: American College Testing Program (about forms submitted to the need analysis servicer)	916-361-0656
College Scholarship Service (CSS)	609-771-7725; TDD 609-883-7051
Need Access/Need Analysis Service	800-282-1550
FAFSA on the WEB Processing/ Software Problems	800-801-0576

Websites

www.ed.gov/prog_info/SFAStudentGuide.
The Student Guide is a free informative brochure about financial aid and is available online at the Department of Education's Web address listed here.

www.ed.gov/prog_info/SFA/FAFSA
This site offers students help in completing the FAFSA.

www.ed.gov/offices/OPE/t4_codes.html.
This site offers a list of Title IV school codes that you may need to complete the FAFSA.

www.ed.gov/offices/OPE/express.html
This site enables you to fill out and submit the FAFSA online. You will need to print out, sign, and send in the release and signature pages.

www.career.org
This is the website of the Career College Association (CCA). It offers a limited number of scholarships for attendance at private proprietary schools. You can also contact CCA at 750 First Street, NE, Suite 900, Washington, DC 20002-4242.

www.salliemae.com
Website for Sallie Mae that contains information about loan programs.

Software Programs

Cash for Class

Tel: 800-205-9581

Fax: 714-673-9039

Redheads Software, Inc.

3334 East Coast Highway #216

Corona del Mar, CA 92625

E-mail: cashclass@aol.com

C-LECT Financial Aid Module

Chronicle Guidance Publications

P.O. Box 1190

Moravia, NY 13118-1190

Tel: 800-622-7284 or 315-497-0330

Fax: 315-497-3359

Peterson's Award Search

Peterson's

P.O. Box 2123

Princeton, NJ 08543-2123

Tel: 800-338-3282 or 609-243-9111

E-mail: custsvc@petersons.com

Pinnacle Peak Solutions (Scholarships 101)

Pinnacle Peak Solutions

7735 East Windrose Drive

Scottsdale, AZ 85260

Tel: 800-762-7101 or 602-951-9377

Fax: 602-948-7603

TP Software—Student Financial Aid Search Software

TP Software

P.O. Box 532

Bonita, CA 91908-0532

Tel: 800-791-7791 or 619-496-8673

E-mail: mail@tpsoftware.com

Books and Pamphlets

Pamphlets

The Student Guide

Published by the U.S. Department of Education, this is the handbook about federal aid programs. To get a printed copy, call 1-800-4-FED-AID.

Looking for Student Aid

Published by the U.S. Department of Education, this is an overview of sources of information about financial aid. To get a printed copy, call 1-800-4-FED-AID.

How Can I Receive Financial Aid for College?

Published from the Parent Brochures ACCESS ERIC website. Order a printed copy by calling 800-LET-ERIC or write to ACCESS ERIC, Research Blvd-MS 5F, Rockville, MD 20850-3172.

Books

Cassidy, Daniel J. *The Scholarship Book 2002: The Complete Guide to Private-Sector Scholarships, Fellowships, Grants, and Loans for the Undergraduate* (Englewood Cliffs, NJ: Prentice-Hall, 2001).

Chany, Kalman A. and Geoff Martz. *Student Advantage Guide to Paying for College 1997 Edition* (NY: Random House, 1997).

College Scholarship Service. *College Costs & Financial Aid Handbook, 18th edition* (NY: The College Entrance Examination Board, 1998).

Cook, Melissa L. *College Student's Handbook to Financial Assistance and Planning* (Traverse City, MI: Moonbeam Publications, Inc., 1991).

Davis, Hern, and Joyce Lain Kennedy. *College Financial Aid for Dummies* (NY: IDG Books Worldwide, 1999).

Davis, Kristen. *Financing College: How to Use Savings, Financial Aid, Scholarships, and Loans to Afford the School of Your Choice* (Washington, DC: Random House, 1996).

Peterson's Guides. *Peterson's Scholarships, Grants and Prizes 2002* (Princeton, NJ: Peterson's, 2001).

Peterson's Guides. *Scholarships, Grants & Prizes: Guide to College Financial Aid from Private Sources* (Princeton, NJ: Peterson's, 2001).

Ragins, Marianne. *Winning Scholarships for College: An Insider's Guide* (New York: Henry Holt & Co., 1994).

Schlacter, Gail, and R. David Weber. *Scholarships 2000* (New York: Kaplan, 1999).

Schwartz, John. *College Scholarships and Financial Aid* (New York: Simon & Schuster, 1995).

Other Related Financial Aid Books

Annual Register of Grant Support (Chicago, IL: Marquis, annual).

A's and B's of Academic Scholarships (Alexandria, VA: Octameron, annual).

Chronicle Student Aid Annual (Moravia, NY: Chronicle Guidance, annual).

College Blue Book. Scholarships, Fellowships, Grants and Loans (New York: Macmillan, annual).

College Financial Aid Annual (New York: Prentice-Hall, annual).

Directory of Financial Aids for Minorities (San Carlos, CA: Reference Service Press, biennial).

Directory of Financial Aids for Women (San Carlos, CA: Reference Service Press, biennial)

Financial Aid for the Disabled and their Families (San Carlos, CA: Reference Service Press, biennial).

Financial Aids for Higher Education (Dubuque, IA: William C. Brown, biennial).

Leider, Robert and Ann. *Don't Miss Out: The Ambitious Student's Guide to Financial Aid* (Alexandria, VA: Octameron, annual).

Peterson's Guides. *Paying Less for College* (Princeton, NJ: Peterson's Guides, annual).

THE INSIDE TRACK

Who:	Lisa Cain
What:	President
	Legal Concierge, Inc.
Where:	Dallas, Texas

INSIDER'S STORY

I got interested in the legal profession as a fluke—I got laid off by a company that I was working for, and when I went to the Unemployment Commission they asked me if becoming a paralegal was a career that I might be interested in, and if so, they would show me how to get started. So, I went for it. I started by looking at all the different paralegal programs in my area, and I chose the best one. After I received my certification, I conducted my job search by networking. I simply walked into firms and begin to build a rapport with someone, anyone that smiled back at me, I would ask who would be the best person to talk to and then leave that person a note that usually said something like, "I came by, and I have an interest in your firm. Would you please take a minute to meet with me?" There are all sorts of job-hunting resources; but I still think networking is the best of all avenues.

Walking right into a place might seem aggressive, but most employers like that attitude in prospective employees, especially in the legal profession. And it worked; I landed a job pretty quickly as a Litigation Paralegal with a prestigious firm.

That first firm that I went to work for threw me onto a huge telecommunications case right away. They let me oversee all of the logistics—taking care of the attorneys' needs, catering, flights, condos, hotels, plus overseeing and dealing with all of the vendors, from copy companies to caterers. It was a fabulous experience, and one that would serve me well in the future.

I recently branched out and started my own business serving other Litigation Paralegals, Attorneys, and Litigation Support Managers at many firms. I now own a business called Legal Concierge, Inc. (www.mylegalconcierge.com). We handle all of the logistics for a trial team getting ready to go to trial. We go into a city and have everything in place before the trial team gets there. We can have the war room set up, all accommodations in place, and all vendors in place, ready to go. We handle everything so that the Trial Paralegals do not have to pull off their positions on the case and take away from their billable hours. Our slogan is *"We focus on the details so that you can focus on the case."*

I would advise anyone interested in becoming a paralegal to go for it, but know that excellent people skills, meticulous organizational skills, quick mental abilities, good common sense, and loyalty are musts for success. I also recommend that new paralegals do an internship or work for temp agencies, as they can be very enlightening as to what kind of law you might want to practice. Be prepared to work hard—working under pressure is a given at most firms; it takes awhile to get really good at what you want to do and patience is a must. But you'll be satisfied in the end. I love my work; there are many perks, and the people that I work with are intelligent and have a lot of interesting experiences to talk about. I like working with sharp people who inspire me to push myself. This profession does that for me.

CHAPTER four

FINDING YOUR FIRST JOB

THIS CHAPTER will take you through the job search process, explaining the many ways to locate a future employer once your paralegal training is completed (and even give you some tips on how you may find a job while still in school). You will learn how to conduct your job search through networking, research, reading industry publications, using classified ads, utilizing online resources, visiting job fairs, and contacting job hotlines. Knowing how to find the best employment opportunities is the first step in the job search process.

NOW THAT you've finished, or nearly finished, the education you need to become a paralegal, you're ready to find employment in your chosen field. The job market outlook is great, according to the U.S. Department of Labor. In their *Occupational Outlook Handbook, 2000–01*, the Bureau of Labor Statistics reports that the paralegal profession will continue to be one of the fastest growing in the country through 2008. However, outpacing job growth is the number of graduates of training programs, meaning you will be facing some serious competition for employment. A healthy dose of confidence will be a real asset: look at the competition as incentive to make yourself the very best job candidate you can be, rather than something to be feared. Aim to land the type of job you really want, rather than taking the first opportunity that comes along.

Think about all the specialties that interest you, and also contemplate the possibility of a job that allows you to gain a wide range of experience through exposure to many areas of the law. Then, think carefully about the type of environment you might feel most comfortable working in. Some of your options include: a large national company with a corporate environment, a small law firm with a family feel, or something in between.

During your paralegal training, you've probably learned about many of these job options, and know how broad the legal employment field is. If you already know the exact type of paralegal position you're looking for, you're ahead of most of your job-searching peers. However, try not to limit your search based on what you think you want. Keeping an open mind while looking for employment can help put you in the running for great job opportunities that you've never considered before.

Even without the competition, the job search process can be time consuming and stressful. But by reading this chapter, you will give yourself an advantage. You will learn how to take an organized approach to the whole procedure, by setting deadlines and staying on top of the details. You will also learn how to find and utilize the best resources available to you, including the Internet, your school's career placement office, and networking contacts.

TAKING A DEADLINE-ORIENTED APPROACH TO YOUR JOB SEARCH EFFORTS

As we've already discussed, landing a job can be a difficult task. You have to find job opportunities, create a resume, write cover letters, schedule interviews, perform research on companies, participate in interviews, make follow up calls, and keep track of all the potential employers you meet or correspond with. One way to help take the stress out of this whole procedure is to adopt an organized, deadline-oriented approach for finding a job as a paralegal.

Begin by purchasing (if you don't already own one) a personal planner, such as a Day-Timer, or a personal digital assistant (PDA), such as a Palm Pilot (www.palm.com). Before actually starting your job search, make a list of everything you will have to accomplish in order to land a job. Break up the big tasks into lots of smaller ones, which are easier to accomplish. Items you will probably put on your list include:

▶ writing or updating your resume

▶ getting your resume printed

▶ purchasing outfits to wear to interviews

▶ following up with interviewers post-interview

Once your list is complete, write down how long you think each task will take to accomplish.

Next, prioritize your list. Determine what tasks need to be done immediately, and which items can wait until later in the job search process. When you know what needs to be done and approximately how long it will take to accomplish each task, create a schedule for yourself and set deadlines.

Using your personal planner, calendar, or PDA, start at today's date and enter in each job search-related task, one at a time. Under your list of tasks to complete, add items like "check the help wanted ads" and "update resume." Leave yourself enough time to accomplish each task, and in your planner, mark down the date by which each task should be completed.

Keep meticulous notes in your planner or on your PDA. Write down everything you do—with whom you make contact, the phone numbers and addresses of your contacts, topics of discussion on the phone or during interviews, the follow up actions that need to be taken, and even what you wore to each interview. Throughout your job search process, keep your planner or PDA with you at all times. Refer to it and update it often to ensure that you remain on-track.

Refer to your planner or PDA during job interviews, and don't be afraid to jot down notes during the interview. If the interviewer wants to meet with you again, take out your planner or PDA, and make the appointment on the spot. Not only will you be organized but you will also demonstrate this important quality to a potential employer.

RESEARCHING THE FIELD

Finding the right job always begins with research. You need to know exactly what paralegal jobs you're qualified to fill, what jobs are available, where the jobs can be found, and how to land one of those jobs. Listed in this chapter are the major employers of paralegals: law firms, corporations, nonprofit organizations, and government agencies; along with resources for finding the information you will want to have about a potential employer.

Law Firms

The *Martindale-Hubbell Law Directory* is a multi-volume set that includes the names, addresses, and phone numbers of all lawyers and law firms in the United States. This information is listed by attorney name, firm name, location, and specialty. The directory also lists lawyers employed by corporations and governments. If your placement office doesn't have a copy, check the nearest law library. You can also access Martindale-Hubbell on the Web at www.martindale.com. West Publishing also maintains an Internet directory of attorneys, called *West's Legal Directory*, at www.wld.com.

Your state, county, or city bar association also compiles a directory of attorneys. In most cases, it will list the lawyers by name and by area of practice. A list of state bar associations may be found in Appendix A at the back of this book, which includes contact information such as e-mail addresses and phone numbers. And don't overlook the phone book as a resource. Most Yellow Pages have a section for "attorneys" or "lawyers" that includes lists by practice area as well as alphabetical lists. Finally, many of your professors probably are or were practicing attorneys, and they may know which firms in your area meet your criteria for an employer.

Corporations

If you are considering work as a corporate paralegal, check the Internet to help you locate potential employers. Listed below are a number of sites that may be useful in finding the information you're looking for, including a company's chief legal officer, description of their legal department, and contact information.

> www.analysiszone.com
> www.businessjeeves.com/MoneyComInd.html
> www.corporateinformation.com
> www.companydescriptions.com
> www.planetbiz.com

Don't forget to check with your school's placement office, which should also have information about corporations that employ paralegals. They may even have contacts with companies that routinely hire their paralegal graduates.

Nonprofit Organizations

There are a variety of directories of nonprofit organizations. On the Internet, check www.nonprofits.org, and *Non-Profit Times'* website, www.nptimes. com. A good national directory is Daniel Lauber's *Non-Profits and Education Job Finder*. If you are involved in a particular cause, as a paralegal or just as a citizen, ask the volunteers and paid staff for ideas on locating other nonprofit organizations that hire paralegals.

Government Agencies

There are thousands of paralegal jobs within the government, at the federal, state, and municipal levels. In order to find out more about the positions available, you will need to know which departments or agencies need or may need the services of paralegals. At the federal level, the Department of Justice is the largest employer, followed by the Departments of Treasury and Defense, and the Federal Deposit Insurance Corporation. You can learn more about them on their websites:

www.usdoj.gov
www.ustreas.gov
www.defenselink.mil
www.fdic.gov

For government positions at the state level, check with your State Job Service office. A list of these offices may be found at jobsearch.about.com/library/ blstatedol.htm. Also, check the section on page 115 entitled Government Job Searches for more ideas about how to find out about paralegal jobs with the government.

FINDING THE JOBS AVAILABLE

There are a number of great ways to locate employment as a paralegal. Some have been around for years, such as classified ads and job placement firms. Others are more recent additions to the job search arena, and offer great possibilities. They include such Internet resources as industry-specific sites, some of which list employment opportunities, and general career-related websites that furnish everything from tips on writing your resume to links to finding jobs in your area.

School Career Placement Centers

Almost every school has a career placement center, whose director has the job of helping you find employment when you graduate. A good placement office will have directories of law firms and other businesses in the local area, information about job fairs, and copies of any industry publications that list paralegal job openings. A top placement director also maintains contacts with the legal and business communities so that your school's placement office will be one of the first places to hear about a job opening and can give you valuable general information about the market in your area.

Temporary Agencies

There are a growing number of agencies around the country that provide temporary legal employees, including attorneys and paralegals, law firms, corporations, and others. While it may at first seem an unlikely first step in your career to sign up with such an agency, it has some advantages. Temporary work gives you the opportunity to gain valuable experience. It also allows you to look over several different workplaces and get an idea of where you'd like to work permanently. And as with an internship, it gives employers a chance to get to know you. Many people gain permanent employment through temporary assignments.

Another advantage to temp work is the wide variety of legal assignments offered to paralegals. Some paralegals enjoy the changes in environment and tasks, and work through temporary agencies for years. Gayle Lund, a litigation paralegal in Los Angeles, got her current, permanent job through a temporary agency.

> In L.A.—I don't know if it was the same around the rest of the country—around 1994 up through mid-1996, law firms were hit very hard by the recession. They were downsizing tremendously, and so there ceased to be an abundance of paralegal jobs. In the graduating class that was just before us there were about 26 people, and every one of them got their job within a month or two of getting their certificate. With our class, that didn't happen. The same goes for the class after us; none of them got full-time jobs for over a year. The economy here was so bad for a while that everyone started going with temp agencies. You get your foot in the door, and if they like you and they need you, they'll hire you.

Lund's first temp job, in 1996, turned into the job she still has today.

Classified Ads

Conventional job-hunting wisdom says you shouldn't depend too much on want ads for finding a job. However, this resource shouldn't be overlooked, especially if you're still in school. By reading the classifieds, you can learn valuable information about the market for paralegals in your area, and you will see at least a partial list of the places that hire paralegals. For instance, a recent edition of a small town newspaper contained an ad from a local hospital for a paralegal—you may not have realized the existence of this market. In the back of this book in Appendix B, you can find sample job descriptions from classified ads, to give you a good idea of how classifieds can be a useful aid in your job search.

You can get other information from the classifieds, such as typical salaries and benefits in your area. One of the hardest questions to answer on an application or in an interview is "What is your desired salary?" If you've been watching the ads, you will have an idea of the going rate. You can also get information about the temporary and part-time jobs. In some areas, temporary and part-time jobs may be a very common way for paralegals to begin their careers.

Aside from the educational aspect of want ads, reading and responding to them may actually lead to a position. Many law firms advertise paralegal positions this way, primarily because it is an inexpensive way to reach a large number of potential applicants. However, that means that, depending on your area, dozens of applicants will send a resume to the employer, and you will be competing with all of them. Don't wait to respond. If the ad appears in the Sunday newspaper, respond to it first thing Monday morning. Used properly, the classifieds cannot only improve your knowledge of the job market, but can lead to your first position as a paralegal.

Job Directories

While the Internet has probably surpassed the library in terms of usefulness in your job search, your local library and chamber of commerce are still very good places to look. Both maintain directories of employers in your area. Two excellent sources organized specifically for job hunters are *The World Almanac National Job Finder's Guide* (St. Martin's Press) and the *Job Bank* series (Adams, Inc.). There are brief job descriptions and online resources in the *Job Finder's Guide*; the *Job Bank* books are published by geographic region and contain a section profiling specific companies, with contact information for major employers in your region sorted by industry. Once you've identified companies in your area of interest, use the resources at your local library to learn more about them. Your librarian can help you find public information about local firms, including the names of all the company's officers, the number of employees, a brief description of the company, and contact information.

Job Placement Firms

Generally speaking, two types of businesses specialize in job placement: employment agencies and contract houses. Employment agencies search for full-time employment opportunities for you. Be sure to find out who is responsible for paying the fee before you sign up with an agency; some charge it to you, while others collect it from your new employer. After you are placed in a job, your relationship with the placement agency ends.

A contract house places you in short- or long-term contract positions for an ongoing fee paid by the employer (example: the employer pays $20 per hour for your skills; you make $15 per hour, and the contract house makes $5 per hour). When your contract with a particular company is over, the contract house finds another contract position for you. You are not an employee of the companies you contract with, and you do not receive benefits from them. An advantage of contracting is that you get a variety of experiences.

To find job placement firms in your area, search the Internet with the terms " 'job placement' and paralegal."

Job Fairs

Attending job or career fairs is another way to find employment. Job fairs bring together a number of employers under one roof, usually at a hotel, convention center, or civic center. These employers send representatives to the fair to inform prospective employees about their company, accept resumes, and occasionally, to conduct interviews for open positions. Many fairs are held specifically for paralegal employers and prospective employees. They usually hold seminars for attendees covering such topics as resume writing, job hunting strategies, and interviewing skills. To find the next scheduled job fair in your area, contact the information office of the convention center or civic center nearest you and ask if a job fair is on their upcoming events calendar. The local newspaper or state unemployment office may have relevant information. And check the Internet with the search terms "job fair and paralegal."

While it's true that you will most likely be competing with many other job seekers at a job fair, your ability to impress an employer is far greater during an in-person meeting than it is if you simply respond to a "help wanted" ad by submitting your resume. By attending a job fair, your appearance, level of preparation, what you say and how you say it, as well as your body language can be used to help make an employer interested in hiring you.

When attending a job fair, your goal is to get invited to come in later for a formal in-person interview. Since you will have limited time with an employer at a job fair, typically between five and ten minutes, it's very rare that an employer will hire someone on the spot, but this does happen.

Preparation on your part is vital. Determine beforehand which employers will be there and whether or not you have the qualifications to fill the job openings available. Begin your research by visiting the website created to promote the job fair you are interested in attending. The website typically lists detailed information about the firms attending and what types of jobs participating employers are looking to fill. Once you pinpoint the firms you're interested in, research them as if you're preparing for an actual in-person job interview.

Determine exactly how your qualifications and skills meet the needs of employers in which you are interested. Also, develop a list of questions to ask the employer during your in-person meeting at the job fair. Showing a sincere interest in working for an employer and asking questions that demonstrate your interest will help set you apart from the competition in a positive way.

Bring plenty of copies of your resume to the job fair. Begin your visit to the job fair by visiting the companies you're most interested in working for. It's best to visit these firms as early in the day as possible, since as the day goes on, the people working the job fair tend to get tired and may be less responsive, especially if they've already met with several dozen potential applicants. You should be prepared to answer questions about why you want to work for that firm and how your skills and qualifications make you qualified to fill one of the positions the employer has available. As you meet with people, collect business cards and follow up your meetings later that day with a short letter, e-mail, or fax, thanking the person you met with for their time. Use this correspondence to reaffirm your interest in working for that employer.

Online Resources

As mentioned previously, one of the fastest growing and most comprehensive resources for job searching is the Internet. There are two types of sites that you should find to be of great use as you look for employment. The first, career-related websites, offer help with every step of the process, from resume writing to researching a firm before accepting a job offer. On some of these sites you may also network with other people in your field, and obtain valuable career-related advice. The second type of site is law-related, and contains lists of job openings geared specifically to the legal profession. You can find a comprehensive list of both types of sites in Appendix B.

Government Job Searches

Finding a job with the government is a more involved process than finding one at a law firm or corporation. While some federal agencies have the authority to test and hire applicants directly, most work through the Office of Personnel Management (OPM), which accepts applications, administers the appropriate written tests, and then submits an eligibility list of qualified candidates to the agency for consideration. For example, if you want a job with The Bureau of Alcohol, Tobacco, and Firearms (ATF), you will have to wait until you see a specific vacancy announcement posted through the OPM, then go through the office to start the application process.

There are several ways to get information from OPM, with the easiest being through their website at www.opm.gov. On this site, you can read answers to frequently asked questions, read about changes that are affecting government employees, read and download or print some of the forms you may need, and get some background information about the OPM. You can also contact them at 912-757-3000, TDD 912-744-2299, or by fax at 912-757-3100.

The OPM also operates www.usajobs.opm.gov, which lists employment opportunities, including the full text of the job announcement. The announcement will give you the classification of the job, known as a "grade." It will indicate the experience necessary, salary level, and other aspects of the job. Once you have read the application process for a specific job, you can access an online application that may be used to create a resume. After creating it, you can submit the resume electronically, or save it to their system to retrieve and edit for future use.

You may also find a paralegal position with the government at many individual government agencies, which do their own hiring and maintain websites that list job openings. *Federal Jobs Digest* maintains a website that claims to be the country's premier source of federal job information. They not only post job openings, but also allow you to register your resume, conduct a job-matching search, and read job descriptions, including the extensive benefits that come with federal employment. Check them out at www.jobsfed.com.

Industry-specific periodicals, such as those listed later in this section, often list federal government job openings, as do national newspapers. If the federal job is in a local area, such as the local office of the Federal Bureau of Investigation, it may be listed in a local newspaper. You may also get information from a Federal Job Information Center. There is at least one of these centers in each state, which posts federal job openings for the area in which it is located. While many offer only a recording over the telephone or several job announcements posted on the wall, they can be a worthwhile contact.

Finally, Federal Reports, Inc. publishes a *Paralegal's Guide to U.S. Government Jobs*. Your placement office may have a copy of this book. If not, you can order it online at www.attorneyjobs.com/attorneyjobs.com/paraguide.html (it costs $23.45, including shipping and handling).

Industry Newsletters & Magazines

Knowing how to stay on top of changes in the paralegal field will help make you a more attractive candidate for any job. One of the best ways to track changes and identify trends in the legal community is by reading newspapers and publications geared toward it. These publications will announce breaking news and explain its significance. Being up on industry news will help convince potential employers that you will be a valuable asset.

If you're already a member of one or more of the three largest paralegal associations (NALA, NFPA, and AAfPE), you're familiar with the publications they produce. If not, they are listed in Appendix B. For more general legal news and industry reporting, check out newsletters put out by your state bar association and/or state paralegal association (search the Internet with the terms "paralegal and newsletter" along with your state). You may also want to read some of the following:

Lexis-Nexis Paralegal Newsletter—www.lexis-nexis.com/paralegal/Newsletters
Legal Assistant Today Magazine—www.jamespublishing.com/books/lat.htm
American Bar Association Journal—www.abanet.org/journal/
The Internet Law Journal—www.tilj.com/content/home.htm

NETWORKING

Networking, the art of making contact with others to obtain information or get help meeting a specific goal, is a major job search tactic used by people in all industries. But no matter how widespread its use, networking remains intimidating to some, who picture it as insincere small talk or handshaking. However, when it is done properly, it is completely sincere, and can provide many benefits, such as:

▶ Mentoring
▶ Making contacts within a hiring firm or company
▶ Furthering training
▶ Getting information about trends in the industry

The key to successful networking is to break down the process into easy-to-follow steps. We will explore these steps below, showing each step's direct application to a paralegal job search.

Step One: Identify Small Goals

Of course your ultimate goal, not only for networking, but also for the entire job search process, is to find a great job. However, you shouldn't approach day-to-day networking as a means to that larger goal. Instead, as your first step, identify smaller goals that can be met quickly. For instance, you have narrowed down your search to three law firms in your area. Now, you want to get "inside" information about these offices in order to decide which to apply for a job with. Or, you may simply be seeking advice from those already working in the field. Once your goals are identified, you can best determine how to meet them.

Step Two: Be Informed

If your goal is to seek advice about corporate law departments in your area, get as much information as you can first. Research the companies that hire paralegals as described above. Understand the paralegal field in general, too. You want to sound like you have done your homework when you begin to make contacts.

This is also the step in which you begin to make a list of potential contacts that may help you meet your goal(s). If you're in school, the person at the job placement office of your school should be at the head of your list. Then, the research you do will probably mention by name the head of a corporate legal department, or hiring partner in a law firm. Newsletters from your state bar and paralegal associations may list paralegals working in your area. The students and teachers you met during your training are also good candidates for this list.

Step Three: Make a Connection

Using the list of potential contacts you developed in step two, build a network of paralegals who work at the offices you are interested in joining. Call them, or visit their offices. Although busy, most agents will take a few minutes to speak with a prospective newcomer. They were new to the business once themselves, so if you are careful not to take up too much of their time, they will probably be glad to give you some information. Begin by introducing yourself, showing that you are informed (step two) and interested in what they have to say. Then, ask if they are willing to help you.

Step Four: Ask for What You Want

If your contact indicates that he or she is willing to help you, be honest and direct about what you want. If your goal is to find out inside information about the office in which a contact works, tell her that you are thinking of applying to work there. Then, ask questions such as:

▶ "How do you like the office?"
▶ "What are the benefits of working here?"
▶ "What is the office atmosphere like?"
▶ "Where else have you worked, and how does this office compare?"

Step Five: Expand Your Network

One of the most valuable pieces of information you can get from a contact is another contact. After you've gotten the information you need to meet your step one goal(s), simply ask if he or she would mind sharing with you the name of another person who might also be able to help you.

Also consider requesting informational interviews at firms that interest you. An informational interview is one in which you meet with someone to find out about the company, and may be an excellent opportunity to:

▶ learn more about how the firm works
▶ gain interview experience
▶ make a contact that might help you get a job in the future

You can also expand your circle of contacts by joining professional organizations while you're still a student. Both the National Association of Legal Assistants and the National Federation of Paralegals have discounted student memberships; most professional organizations do so as well. Be sure to join both national organizations and their local chapters. Though the national organizations can give you valuable information, it's on the local level that you will be more effective at networking. Go to local meetings and ask questions—people almost always like to talk about their jobs—and volunteer for committees. The members of your local paralegal group will most likely know about job openings before anyone else does.

Step Six: Organize Yourself

You have probably already written down your goals, and made lists of contacts. Once you've spoken with some of them, organization becomes even more important. You will need to keep track of your contacts, as well as the information you receive from them. When you need to connect with this person again in the future, you will be able to easily access your information. There are software packages that can help you to keep track of your networking contacts, or, you can simply use a notebook and organize yourself.

For each contact, note:

▶ Name
▶ Address
▶ E-mail address
▶ Phone number (work, pager, cellular phone, residence)
▶ Fax number
▶ Company name
▶ Job title
▶ First meeting—where, when, the topics you discussed
▶ Last contact—when, why, and how

Step Seven: Maintain Your Contacts

It is important to maintain your contacts once you have established them. Try to reach people again within a couple of weeks of meeting them. You can send a note of thanks, ask a question, or send a piece of information related to your conversation with them. This contact cements your meeting in their minds, so they will remember you more readily when you call them again in the future. If you haven't communicated with your contacts for a few months, you might send them a note or e-mail about an article you read, or relevant new technology or law to keep your name fresh in their minds.

Gayle Lund feels that as a group, paralegals are good at networking and supporting one another. "The ones I've known have networked quite a bit. In fact, they all keep lists of agencies at which you can get jobs, and they share them with each other. They call each other and tell each other about jobs, and they belong to the associations." She adds that many paralegals volunteer, "partly to learn and partly to network. If you're doing volunteer work, it looks good on your resume and you meet people. A lot of [paralegals] have gone on to get good jobs through the people they met" through volunteer work.

As you begin your job hunt, keep in mind that you are not just looking for a job; you're looking for a good job, one you will enjoy and feel challenged by. Once you've finished paralegal school and an internship, you have much to offer to any legal employer. Remember: you're not begging for a job; you're trying to find an employer who will be a match for your skills and talents.

THE INSIDE TRACK

Who:	Jessica Beckett
What:	Law Student and Former Legal Assistant
Where:	O'Melveny & Myers
	San Francisco, California

INSIDER'S STORY

After I graduated from Brown University in Providence, Rhode Island, I had the itch to leave the East Coast where I was born and raised, and head out west, so I packed everything up and moved to San Francisco. At that time I was pretty much set on becoming an attorney, but I wanted to be absolutely sure before I made the commitment to go to law school. I also wanted to take a year or so off before I returned to school; being a paralegal seemed like the best way to go—I thought I could make some contacts and also learn what it was like to work at a law firm. The only problem was that I lacked real office experience, which is what many firms look for in paralegals. I learned very quickly that I had to play up the research and organizational skills that I used in college. My earliest interviews were disasters, but with each consecutive interview that I went on, I learned a bit more, until I was finally fully prepared to impress my interviewer. I think interviewing with law firms is probably one of the hardest things to do because often you are interviewed by attorneys, and many of them make you feel you are be cross-examined. If you're not prepared, they'll know right away.

I started off my job-hunting process by posting my resume on Monster.com, and I got a couple of responses. For me though, networking seemed to work the best. My father is an attorney so through him it was easy for me to find people at local firms. Once I had some names, I contacted them and asked if I could talk to them on the phone to learn more about working at a law firm. Once I felt comfortable with them, I asked if they were hiring and usually sent them a copy of my resume. I got several interviews this way. Eventually I found my job through someone I knew at a firm who told me they were hiring. I was hired as a paralegal in the Transactional Department at O'Melveny & Myers in San Francisco. I did mostly corporate and real estate work.

My work was standard paralegal stuff: Preparing closing binders at the end of a deal; organizing documents in preparation for a closing; organizing files of documents for storage after a deal; preparing the closing room for the day of execution, drafting agreements and contacting the clients to get documents. In the corporate work, I frequently had to prepare tables that reflected stock options or shares and figure out what percentage of shares various parties owned. This involved quite a bit of work with math. It wasn't the most exciting work. To be honest, sometimes I found the work incredibly boring. At times I wished the attorneys would give me more challenging projects that required more thought and analysis, but until the attorneys really trust you, you will spend most of your time putting together closing binders and organizing filed documents. This can be very tedious, but it's important work, and has to be done. The satisfying thing is that if you develop a good working relationship with an attorney, you can end up doing the work of a first- or second-year attorney as a paralegal, which is exciting and more challenging. For me, that was important because it solidified my decision to go to law school.

I would recommend being a paralegal to anyone in my position. Working as a paralegal at a firm really gives you a clear idea of whether or not you are cut out to be an attorney. For me it was a positive experience—I will be attending the law school at UC Hastings in San Francisco this fall.

CHAPTER five

JOB SEARCH SKILLS: RESUME AND COVER LETTER WRITING; INTERVIEWING

ONCE YOU'VE pinpointed the job opportunities you're interested in pursuing, you will need to contact your potential employer to express your interest. The way you make that contact can be just as important as your skills and training. This chapter will help make sure the impression you leave is the very best possible, making you stand out as a superior candidate above the competition, and putting you on your way to employment.

YOUR FIRST contact with a potential employer may be through a phone call, a mailed cover letter and resume, an e-mailed resume, or an interview. Whatever the form, it is imperative that you use it to make an excellent impression. A resume with spelling errors, an unprofessional sounding phone call, or an interview where you arrive ten minutes late can be a disaster to a job search. It's not hard to master the job search skills you need to succeed, but it does take some time and effort. By carefully reading this chapter, you will learn how to land the job you want by writing great cover letters and resumes, and interviewing with confidence and proficiency.

WRITING YOUR RESUME

Whether you are responding to an advertisement, following up on a networking opportunity, or making a cold contact, your resume is usually the first means by which a potential employer learns about you. Think of it as an advertisement you write to help sell yourself. A successful advertisement catches attention by combining several elements: content, composition, clarity, and concentration. Falling short in any of these areas can cause a reader to pass over the ad; you want to make sure that a prospective employer will pay attention to yours.

As you write, edit, and proofread your resume, make an effort to keep all of the information short, to the point, and totally relevant. Anything you leave out can be discussed later, during a job interview. The purpose of your resume is to get an employer interested enough in you so you make it to the next level—getting invited for an interview.

Creating a powerful resume will take time and effort. Even if you've written dozens before, it is worth your while to seek out good resume-writing resources to help you draft one for your new paralegal career. While much has remained the same over the years, there are current standards and trends for resumes, including e-mailed and computer scannable resumes, that you should know about. To start, check out your school's placement office, which may have copies of former students' paralegal resumes. Books such as *Great Resume* by Jason R. Rich (LearningExpress, 2000) contain excellent general guidelines. And there are plenty of online resources to help you create a winning resume, including the following:

- ABA Resume Writing—www.abastaff.com/career/resume/resume.htm
- Accent Resume Writing—www.accent-resume-writing.com/critiques
- Creative Professional Resumes—www.resumesbycpr.com
- First Resume Store International—www.resumestore.com
- Free Resume Tips—www.free-resume-tips.com
- Professional Association of Resume Writers—www.parw.com/homestart.html
- Proven Resumes—www.provenresumes.com
- Rebecca Smith's eResumes & Resources—www.eresumes.com

▶ Resumania—www.resumania.com

▶ Resume Broadcaster—www.resumebroadcaster.com

▶ Resume Magic—www.liglobal.com/b_c/career/res.shtml

▶ Resume Plus—www.resumepls.com

▶ Resume.com—www.resume.com

▶ Resumedotcom—www.resumedotcom.com

▶ The Confident Resume—www.tcresume.com

▶ The Resume—www.wm.edu/csrv/career/stualum/resmdir/contents.htm

In addition to the above list of websites, there are many more career-related websites listed in Appendix B that also offer resume-writing tips. The four most important elements of resume writing: content, composition, clarity, and concentration are discussed next.

Content

Use the questionnaire below to gather the information you will need for your resume. In the following sections, you will learn how best to organize, format, and word your resume to make the best possible impression.

Contact Information

The only personal information that belongs on your resume is your name (on every page, if your resume exceeds one page in length), address, phone number, fax number, and e-mail address (if you have them). Under no circumstances should you include personal information such as age, gender, religion, health, marital status, or number of children.

Full name:_____

Permanent street address:_____

City, state, zip:_____

Daytime telephone number:_____

Evening telephone number:_____

Pager/cell phone number (optional):_____

Fax number (optional):_____

E-mail address:_____

Personal website address/online portfolio URL:_____

School Address (if applicable):_____

Your phone number at school (if applicable):_____

Job/Career Objective(s)

Write a short description of the job you're seeking. Be sure to include as much information as possible about how you can use your skills to the employer's benefit. Later, you will condense this answer into one short sentence.

_____

_____

_____

What is the job title you're looking to fill? (i.e. paralegal)_____

_____

Educational Background

Be sure to include your internships in this section. For most recent graduates, it is their only legal experience and perhaps their only work experience. Include the skills you learned which will be applicable to the position for which you're applying.

List the most recent college or university you've attended:_____

City/state:_____

What year did you start?:_____

Graduation month/year:_____

Degree(s) and/or award(s) earned:_____

Your major:_____

Your minor(s):_____

List some of your most impressive accomplishments, extracurricular activities, club affiliations, etc.:_____

List computer courses you've taken that help qualify you for the job you're seeking:_____

_____

_____

Grade point average (GPA):_____

Other colleges/universities you've attended:_____

City/state:_____

What year did you start?:_____

Graduation month/year:_____

Degree(s) and/or award(s) earned:_____

Your major:_____

Your minor(s):_____

List some of your most impressive accomplishments, extracurricular activities, club affiliations, etc.:_____

_____

List computer courses you've taken that help qualify you for the job you're seeking:_____

_____

_____

Grade point average (GPA):_____

High school attended:_____

City/state:_____

Graduation date:_____

Grade point average (GPA)_____

List the names and phone numbers of one or two current or past professors/teachers (or guidance counselors) you can contact about obtaining a letter of recommendation or list as a reference:_____

_____

_____

Personal Skills and Abilities

Your *personal skill set* (the combination of skills you possess) is something that differentiates you from everyone else. Skills that are marketable in the workplace aren't always taught in school, however. Your ability to manage people, stay cool under pressure, remain organized, surf the Internet, use software applications, speak in public, communicate well in writing, communicate in multiple languages, or perform research, are all examples of marketable skills.

When reading job descriptions or "help wanted" ads, pay careful attention to the wording used to describe what the employer is looking for. As you customize your resume for a specific employer, you will want to match up what the employer is looking for with your own qualifications as closely as possible. Try to utilize the wording provided by the employer within the classified ad or job description.

What do you believe is your most marketable skill? Why?_____

_____

_____

List three or four specific examples of how you have used this skill in the past while at work. What was accomplished as a result?

1._____

2._____

3._____

4._____

What are keywords or buzzwords that can be used to describe your skill?_____

_____

What is another of your marketable skills?_____

Provide at least three examples of how you've used this skill in the workplace:

1._____

2._____

3._____

What unusual or unique skill(s) do you possess that help you stand out from other applicants applying for the same types of positions as you?

_____

_____

How have you already proven this skill is useful in the workplace?

_____

What computer skills do you possess?_____

What computer software packages are you proficient in (such as Microsoft Office—Word, Excel, PowerPoint, FrontPage, etc.)?_____

_____

_____

Thinking carefully, what skills do you believe you currently lack?

_____

What skills do you have, but that need to be polished or enhanced in order to make you a more appealing candidate? _____

_____

What options are available to you to either obtain or brush up on the skills you believe need improvement (for example: evening/weekend classes at a college or university, adult education classes, seminars, books, home study courses, on-the-job-training, etc.):_____

_____

_____

In what time frame could you realistically obtain this training?

_____

_____

Work/Employment History

Previous work experience is very important. Even if it had nothing to do with the legal field, every job taught you something that will make you a better legal assistant. Careers such as medicine, accounting, real estate, human resources, and insurance, as well as many others, will be considered hiring pluses by potential employers. Don't overlook or discount volunteer work for the same reason. You gained skills and experience, and your volunteering also indicates that you are committed to your community. (Keep this in mind as you go through your paralegal training; if you are short on experience, you might think about volunteering.)

Complete the employment-related questions below for all of your previous employers, including part-time or summer jobs held while in school, as well as temp jobs, internships, and volunteering. You probably won't want to reveal your past earning history to a potential employer, but you may want this information available as reference when you begin negotiating your future salary, benefits, and overall compensation package.

Most recent employer:_____
City/state:_____
Year you began work:_____
Year you stopped working (write "present" if still employed):_____
Job title:_____
Job description:_____

_____

Reason for leaving:_____
What were your three proudest accomplishments while holding this job?
  1. _____
  2. _____
  3. _____

Contact person at the company who can provide a reference:_____

Contact person's phone number:_____

Annual salary earned:_____

Employer:_____

City/state:_____

Year you began work:_____

Year you stopped working (write "present" if still employed):_____

Job title:_____

Job description:_____

_____

Reason for leaving:_____

What were your three proudest accomplishments while holding this job?

    1. _____

    2. _____

    3. _____

Contact person at the company who can provide a reference:_____

Contact person's phone number:_____

Annual salary earned:_____

Military Service (if applicable)

Branch served in:_____

Years served:_____

Highest rank achieved:_____

Decorations or awards earned:_____

Special skills or training you obtained:_____

Professional Accreditations and Licenses

List any and all of the professional accreditations and/or licenses you have earned thus far in your career. Be sure to highlight items that directly relate to the job(s) you will be applying for:

_____

_____

Hobbies and Special Interests

You may have life experience that should be emphasized for legal employers. Did you help a spouse in a business? Were you a candidate for public office?

Any number of experiences can add to your attractiveness as a paralegal candidate. If you don't have a great deal of work experience, this part of your resume is very important. Think about the things you've done which have taught you lessons that are valuable for a paralegal to know. If you can't find a way to include those experiences on your resume, mention them in your cover letter.

List any hobbies or special interests you have that are not necessarily work-related, but that potentially could separate you from the competition. Can any of the skills utilized in your hobby be adapted for the workplace?

_____

_____

_____

What non-professional clubs or organizations do you belong to or actively participate in?

_____

_____

_____

Personal/Professional Ambitions

You may not want to share these on your resume, but answering the questions below will help you to focus your search, and prepare for possible interviewing topics.

What are your long-term goals?

Personal: _____

Professional: _____

Financial: _____

For your personal, professional, and then financial goals, what are five smaller, short-term goals you can begin working toward achieving right now that will help you ultimately achieve each of your long-term goals?

Short-term personal goals:

1. _____

2. _____

3. _____

4. _____

5. _____

Short-term professional goals:

1. _____
2. _____
3. _____
4. _____
5. _____

Short-term financial goals:

1. _____
2. _____
3. _____
4. _____
5. _____

Will the job(s) you will be applying for help you achieve your long-term goals and objectives? If "yes," how? If "no," why not? _____
_____
_____
_____

Describe your personal, professional, and financial situation right now:
_____
_____
_____

What would you most like to improve about your life overall? _____
_____
_____
_____

What are a few things you can do, starting immediately, to bring about positive changes in your personal, professional, or financial life? _____
_____
_____
_____

Where would you like to be personally, professionally, and financially five and ten years down the road? _____
_____
_____
_____

What needs to be done to achieve these long-term goals or objectives?

_____

_____

_____

_____

What are some of the qualities about your personality that you're most proud of? _____

_____

_____

_____

What are some of the qualities about your personality that you believe need improvement? _____

_____

_____

What do others most like about you? _____

_____

_____

What do you think others least like about you? _____

_____

_____

If you decided to pursue additional education, what would you study and why? How would this help you professionally? _____

_____

_____

_____

If you had more free time, what would you spend it doing? _____

_____

_____

_____

List several accomplishments in your personal and professional life that you're most proud of. Why did you choose these things?

1. _____

2. _____

3. _____

4. _____

5. _____

What were your strongest and favorite subjects in school? Is there a way to incorporate these interests into the job(s) or career path you're pursuing?

_____

_____

_____

What do you believe is your biggest weakness? Why wouldn't an employer hire you? _____

_____

_____

What would be the ideal atmosphere for you to work in? Do you prefer a large corporate atmosphere, working at home, or working in a small office?

_____

_____

_____

List five qualities about a new job that would make it the ideal employment opportunity for you:

1. _____

2. _____

3. _____

4. _____

5. _____

What did you like most about the last place you worked? _____

_____

What did you like least about the last place you worked? _____

_____

What work-related tasks are you particularly good at? _____

_____

_____

What type of coworkers would you prefer to have? _____

_____

_____

When it comes to work-related benefits and perks, what's most important to you? _____

_____

_____

_____

When you're recognized for doing a good job at work, how do you like to
be rewarded? _____

_____

_____

If you were to write a "help wanted" ad describing your "dream job," what
would the ad say? _____

_____

_____

Composition

How your resume looks can be as important as what it says. Potential
employers may receive a stack of resumes for one job opening, and they
probably spend less than one minute deciding which to review further and
which to throw away. Keeping in mind that the legal field is a conservative
one, you will want to achieve an overall look that does not stand out, but
rather is neat, clean, and within standard resume guidelines.

Use the tips in the box below to help organize the material you gathered
in the questionnaire above.

Resume Creation Tips

No matter what type of resume you're putting together, use these tips and strategies to ensure
your finished document has the most impact possible when a potential employer reads it.

- Always use standard letter-size paper in ivory, cream, or another neutral color.
- Include your name, address, and phone number on every page.
- Make sure your name is larger than everything else on the page (example: your
  name in 14-point font, the rest in 12-point).
- Use a font that is easy to read, such as 12-point Times New Roman.
- Do not use more than three fonts in your resume.
- Edit, edit, edit! Read it forward and backward, and then have friends with good
  proofreading skills read it. Don't rely heavily on grammar and spell checkers,
  which can miss errors.
- Use bullet points for items in a list—they highlight your main points, making them
  hard to miss.
- Use key words from the legal field.

- Avoid using excessive graphics such as boxes, distracting lines, and complex designs.
- Be consistent when using bold, capitalization, underlining, and italics. If one company name is underlined, make sure all are underlined. Check titles, dates, and so on.
- Don't list your nationality, race, religion, or gender. Keep your resume as neutral as possible. Your resume is a summary of your skills and abilities.
- Don't put anything personal on your resume such as your birth date, marital status, height, or hobbies.
- One page is best, but do not crowd your resume. Shorten the margins if you need more space; if it's necessary to create a two-page resume, make sure you balance the information on each page. Don't put just one section on the second page. Be careful about where the page break occurs.
- Keep your resume updated. Don't write "9/97 to present" if you ended your job two months ago. Do not cross out or hand-write changes on your resume.
- Understand and remember everything written on your resume. Be able to back up all statements with specific examples.

You can organize the information on your resume in a number of ways, depending on your work history, and how the hiring firm wants the resume submitted. The three most common formats are:

▶ Chronological format
▶ Skills format (also known as a functional resume)
▶ Combination of chronological and skills format

The most common resume format is chronological—you summarize your work experience year-by-year, beginning with your current or most recent employment experience and working backward. For each job, list the dates you were employed, the name and location of the company for which you worked, and the position(s) you held. Work experience is followed by education, which is also organized chronologically.

The skills resume (also known as the functional resume) emphasizes what you can do rather than what you have done. It is useful if you have large gaps in your work history or have relevant skills that would not be properly highlighted in a chronological listing of jobs. The skills resume concentrates on your skills and qualifications. Specific jobs you've held are listed, but they are not the primary focus of this type of resume.

You may decide a combination of the chronological and skills resume would be best to highlight your skills. A combination resume allows for a mixture of your skills with a chronological list of jobs you've held. You get the best of both resumes. This is an excellent choice for students who have limited work experience and who want to highlight specific skills.

Making Your Resume Computer-Friendly

One of the biggest trends in terms of corporate recruiting is for employers to accept resumes online via e-mail, through one of the career-related websites, or via their own website. If you're going to be applying for jobs online or submitting your resume via e-mail, you will need to create an electronic resume (in addition to a traditional printed resume).

Many companies scan all resumes from job applicants using a computer software program with optical character recognition (OCR), and then enter them into a database, where they can be searched using keywords. When e-mailing your electronic resume directly to an employer, as a general rule, the document should be saved in an ASCII, Rich Text, or plain text file. Contact the employer directly to see which method is preferred.

When sending a resume via e-mail, the message should begin as a cover letter (and contain the same information as a cover letter). You can then either attach the resume file to the e-mail message or paste the resume text within the message. Be sure to include your e-mail address and well as your regular mailing address and phone number(s) within all e-mail correspondence. Never assume an employer will receive your message and simply hit "respond" using their e-mail software to contact you.

Guidelines for Creating an Electronic Resume to Be Saved and Submitted in ASCII Format

- Set the left and right margins on the document so that 6.5 inches of text will be displayed per line. This will insure that the text won't automatically wrap to the next line (unless you want it to).
- Use a basic, 12-point text font, such as Courier or Times New Roman.

■ Avoid using bullets or other symbols. Instead, use an asterisk (*) or a dash (-). Instead of using the percentage sign (%) for example, spell out the word *percent*.

■ Use the spell-check feature of the software used to create your electronic resume and then proofread the document carefully. Just as applicant tracking software is designed to pick out keywords from your resume that showcase you as a qualified applicant, these same software packages used by employers can also instantly count the number of typos and spelling errors in your document and report that to an employer as well.

■ Avoid using multiple columns, tables, or charts within your document.

■ Within the text, avoid abbreviations—spell everything out. For example, use the word "Director," not "Dir." or "Vice President" as opposed to "VP." In terms of degrees, however, it's acceptable to use term like "MBA," "B.A.," "Ph.D.," and so on.

Properly formatting your electronic resume is critical to having it scanned or read properly; however, it's what you say within your resume that will ultimately get you hired. According to Rebecca Smith, author of *Electronic Resumes & Online Networking* (Career Press, 2nd Edition) and companion website (www.eresumes.com), "Keywords are the basis of the electronic search and retrieval process. They provide the context from which to search for a resume in a database, whether the database is a proprietary one that serves a specific purpose, or whether it is a Web-based search engine that serves the general public. Keywords are a tool to quickly browse without having to access the complete text. Keywords are used to identify and retrieve a resume for the user.

"Employers and recruiters generally search resume databases using keywords—nouns and phrases that highlight technical and professional areas of expertise, industry-related jargon, projects, achievements, special task forces, and other distinctive features about a prospect's work history."

The emphasis is not on trying to second-guess every possible keyword a recruiter may use to find your resume. Your focus is on selecting and organizing your resume's content in order to highlight those keywords for a variety of online situations. The idea is to identify all possible keywords that are appropriate to your skills and accomplishments that support the kind of jobs you are looking for. But to do that, you must apply traditional resume writing principles to the concept of extracting those keywords from your resume. Once you have written your resume, then you can identify your strategic keywords based on how you imagine people will search for your resume.

The keywords you incorporate into your resume should support or be relevant to your job objective. Some of the best places within your resume to incorporate keywords are when listing:

▶ Job titles
▶ Responsibilities
▶ Accomplishments
▶ Skills

Industry-related buzzwords, job-related technical jargon, licenses, and degrees are among the other opportunities you will have to come up with keywords to add to your electronic resume. If you are posting your resume on the Internet, look for the categories that websites use and make sure you use them too. Be sure the word "paralegal" appears somewhere on your resume, and use accepted professional jargon. Don't, for example, write that you are interested in doing trial work. Someone scanning your resume will probably look for the word "litigation" instead.

For scanned resumes, "manager" is a better bet than "managed." Verbs such as "initiated," "inspired," and "directed" probably won't be keywords either. However, you can still use them—just be sure they aren't taking the place of other possible keywords, or can't be substituted with other possible keywords.

Keywords are often connected by "and" rather than "or." If an employer is looking for someone interested in being a litigation paralegal in a criminal law firm, your resume won't come up if it only contains "litigation paralegal" and not "criminal." It may be helpful to look at some of the resumes posted on the Internet; think about the keywords you use to search for them. The successful hits you get will indicate the words you should be using.

An excellent resource for helping you select the best keywords to use within your electronic resume is the *Occupational Outlook Handbook* (published by the U.S. Department of Labor). This publication is available, free of charge, online (stats.bls.gov/oco/oco1000.htm), however, a printed edition can also be found at most public libraries.

Clarity

No matter how attractive your resume is, it won't do any good if a prospective employer finds it difficult to read. The most important rule of resume writing is: Never send out a resume that contains mistakes. Proofread it several times and use your spell-check. For most people, writing a resume is an ongoing process, so remember to check it over every time you make a change. There is absolutely no excuse for sending out a resume with misspelled words or grammatical errors. After you proofread it, ask one or two friends to read it over too. If you are uncertain about a grammatical construction, for example, change it.

In addition to checking spelling and grammar, you want to make sure that your resume is well written. Resume writing is quite different from other kinds of writing, and it takes some practice. For one thing, most resumes don't use complete sentences. Don't write, "As manager of the housewares department, I managed 14 employees and was in charge of ordering $2.5 million worth of merchandise annually." Do write, "Managed $2.5 million housewares department with 14 employees." Still, all the other rules of grammar apply to writing a resume. Tenses and numbers need to match, and double negatives and other awkward construction are not acceptable.

It is also important to be concise, to help keep your resume at a manageable size, and make the most important information stand out. In the two examples in the above paragraph, the first requires 23 words; the second, just eight. They convey the same information, but the second does it more efficiently. By being concise and demonstrating good word choice, you highlight the fact that you have skills that are highly valued by legal employers. Having excellent communication and organization abilities are vital in the law field, and both can easily be reflected in your resume.

You demonstrate your communication abilities not only by making sure everything is spelled correctly and is grammatically accurate, but also by how well you write your resume. Word choice contributes to the clarity and persuasiveness of your resume. Experts have long recommended using verbs (action words) rather than nouns to promote yourself in a resume. Compare "managed $2.5 million housewares department with 14 employees" to "manager of housewares department." The first sounds much more impressive.

However, there is now one caveat to the verb preference rule. As we discussed above, computer resumes, whether scanned or e-mailed, are searched using keywords. These words tend to be nouns rather than verbs. So, when writing this type of resume, follow the keyword guidelines spelled out on pages 138–139.

Concentration

Each time you send out a resume, whether in response to an ad, following up a networking lead, or even a cold contact, you should concentrate on tailoring your approach for the employer you are contacting. This means having more than one resume, or reconfiguring your resume before printing it so that it conforms better to the job opening to which you're applying. For instance, if you're interested in work as a civil litigation paralegal, but you've got work experience that you enjoyed at an insurance firm, you're looking first for a position in insurance litigation. But, you might also be willing to take a position in the human resources office of an insurance company or anywhere in a large firm that does insurance work, just to get your foot in the door. Insurance litigation is your dream job; the others are your close-to-dream jobs. And if enough time passes, you will be happy to take any litigation position in any kind of office. To apply for all of these jobs, you will need to alter your resume at least three times.

The resume for the insurance litigation job will stress your prior work experience, the litigation skills you learned at your internship, and how well you did in civil procedure in paralegal school. Although it depends on the format you are using, you may very well stress them in that order. For a litigation position in a large firm that handles insurance, you'd probably stress your internship and education—but make sure your insurance experience stands out too. For the human resources job, you'd emphasize your insurance experience and any employment law classes or experience. Finally, for the basic entry-level job, you'd want to construct your resume to show that you are a generalist.

Most books that tell you how to write a resume include advice about the information you should gather before you start. If you keep all of that information at hand, it won't be too difficult to construct a resume that targets a particular job and that concentrates your information so that a prospective employer will see that you are a likely candidate for this opening. In many cases, a few changes to a basic resume are enough to make it appropriate for a particular job opening.

A good way to tailor your resume for a particular opening is to imagine what the job would be like. Imagine, based on the description of the job, the major things you will be expected to do day to day. Then look at your experience and education and decide how to present your information so that the employer will know that you are capable of doing those tasks.

Finally, make sure you get your resume to the appropriate person in the appropriate way. If you got the person's name through a networking contact, your contact may deliver it or suggest that you deliver it in person; most likely, though, you should mail it. If you are making a cold contact—that is, if you are contacting a firm that you found through your research but that is not actively looking to fill a position—make sure you find out the name of the hiring partner or head of the paralegal department and send your resume to them. If you are responding to an ad, make sure you do what the ad says. If it directs you to fax your resume, do so. If it asks for a writing sample, make sure you include one. (If you are using a sample you wrote on a job or internship, you must black out all names and any other identifying information.) Demonstrate your ability to attend to detail.

Avoid Making These Common Resume Errors

- Stretching the truth. A growing number of employers are verifying all resume information. If you're caught lying, you won't be offered a job, or you could be fired later if it's discovered that you weren't truthful.

- Including any references to money. This includes past salary or how much you're looking to earn within your resume and cover letter.

- Including on your resume the reasons why you stopped working for an employer, switched jobs, or are currently looking for a new job. Do not include a line in your resume saying, "Unemployed" or "Out of Work" along with the corresponding dates in order to fill a time gap.

- Having a typo or grammatical error in a resume. If you refuse to take the time necessary to proofread your resume, why should an employer assume you'd take the time needed to do your job properly if you're hired?

■ Using long paragraphs to describe past work experience. Consider using a bulleted list instead. Most employers will spend less than one minute initially reading a resume.

The following are two sample resumes. The first is for an applicant who wants to highlight his previous experience as a tax preparer, as well as his educational background. The second is for an applicant who has more education than experience.

Steve Smith

1234 Broadway

Mytown, ST 00000

Phone and fax: 007-555-5678

E-mail: steve89@online.com

OBJECTIVE:	To work as a paralegal in a position that allows me to utilize and enhance my specialized computer skills and tax preparation experience.

EXPERIENCE

September–December 1999	Paralegal Intern Zelda County Attorney's Office 180 West Main Street, Mytown, ST 00000 007-555-3456
Duties:	Answered multi-line telephones, greeted the public, assisted with filing of pleadings, shepherded cases, filed documents
January 1992–April 1999	Tax Consultant H & R BLOCK 1440 Ivy Road Mytown, ST 00000 007-555-1040
Duties:	Interviewed clients, prepared individual income tax returns, including out-of-state returns, researched and applied IRS rules and regulations
January 1991–Present	Volunteer Dogs and Cats Shelter RR 1 Mytown, ST 00000 007-555-9876
Duties:	Interview adopters, write column for newsletter, bathe dogs
EDUCATION	Associate of Art, Paralegal Studies, May 2000 Paralegal College, 7890 Troubadour Street, Mytown, ST 00000 Associate of Science, Computer Technology, May 1998 Community College, Eli Hills Campus, Mytown, ST 00000
SKILLS	Fluent in Spanish

Jane Jones

521 East Avenue

Mytown, ST 00000

Phone and fax: 007-555-1234

Email: jjones@online.com

OBJECTIVE:	Entry-level paralegal position that allows me to utilize and enhance my specialized computer skills and paralegal education.
EDUCATION	Associate of Art, Paralegal Studies, May 2001
	Paralegal College, 7890 Troubadour Street, Mytown, ST 00000
	Associate of Science, Computer Technology, December 1999
	Community College, Eli Hills Campus, Mytown, ST 00000
	Relevant Courses:
PARALEGAL	Legal Research and Writing
	Business Law
	Litigation
	Family Law
	Criminal Law
COMPUTER TECHNOLOGY	Lotus 123r4
	QBASIC
	DBASE IV
	WordPerfect
	QUICKBOOKS QUICKPAY

EXPERIENCE

September–December 2000	Paralegal Intern, Johnson, Watson, & Partners, 33 Elm Street, Mytown, ST 00000; 007-555-7864
Duties:	Assisted partner by scheduling meetings, events, and appointments
	Filed pleadings
	Performed legal research on CD-ROM, online, and in the library
	Wrote legal memorandum
	Shepherded cases
	Updated website
September 1997–August 1999	Sales Associate, The Store, 345 Route 66, Mytown, ST 00000, 007-555-6543
Duties:	Operated cash register
	Stocked shelves
	Assisted customers

WRITING COVER LETTERS

Never send out a resume without a cover letter. The cover letter aims your resume directly at the available job; your resume, in turn, describes in detail why you are the person for the job. If your cover letter is a failure, your resume might never get looked at by the hiring manager. Your cover letter should give the impression that you may be a good candidate for the job. The four elements of the resume—composition, clarity, content, and concentration—apply to cover letters as well. However, because the cover letter has a different function, these elements have some different functions as well.

Composition

Your cover letter needs to grab the attention of the reader, while remaining within the conservative guidelines discussed above. As with your resume, avoid fancy fonts and stationery; choose something that matches or coordinates with your resume. Your cover letter should always be typed (printed) on good paper, using letterhead with your name, address, phone and fax numbers, and e-mail address. You can make letterhead stationery on your computer rather than ordering it through a printing company.

A cover letter should be composed as you would a business letter. It should include your address (preferably in the letterhead), the date, the name and address of the person the letter is to be sent to, and a salutation. At the end of the body of the letter, include a closing (such as "Sincerely"), your signature, and your name typed out below. You may use block paragraphs or choose to indent them. It is acceptable to type "enclosure" at the bottom, indicating there is material (your resume) enclosed with the letter.

Rarely do you need a cover letter that is more than one page. On occasion, an advertisement for a job will ask for a resume and a detailed statement of interest (or words to that effect). Sometimes ads will even ask you to address specific questions or issues in your letter, such as your goals, or what you can contribute to the organization. In such cases, you may need to write a letter that is more than one page. Normally, however, you can say all that is necessary on one page.

Clarity

As with your resume, never send out a cover letter with a grammatical or spelling error. Even when you are pressed for time and rushing to get a letter out, make sure to spell-check it and proofread it carefully. Ask someone else to look it over as well. Your letter should be accurate, clear, and concise. It serves as a letter of introduction, an extension of your advertisement, and needs to convince a prospective employer that you should be interviewed for the position.

Begin your cover letter with an introduction, followed by an explanation of why you are right for this job, and a closing paragraph. As with your resume, it is vital that your cover letter be well written; however, it requires a different writing style. Sentence fragments don't work in a cover letter.

While a resume offers a somewhat formal presentation of your background, a cover letter should let some of your personality come through. View it as your first chance to speak with a prospective employer. The resume tells employers what you know and what you can do; the cover letter should tell them a little bit about who you are. However, even though it is somewhat less formal, don't use a conversational tone. For example, don't use contractions or slang.

Content and Concentration

While it is important that your resume be tailored to specific job openings, it's even more important to target your cover letter. In fact, its major component should be its concentration on the particular job opening to which you're applying. Because it is so specific, you will need to write a new cover letter every time you send out your resume. It should never read like a form letter, nor should it just repeat the information in your resume. It tells the prospective employer why you are the one for the job.

In the first paragraph, indicate why you are writing the letter at this time. You may write something like:

▶ "I would like to apply for the litigation paralegal position advertised in the April 11 *Sunday Post*."

▶ "I am writing in response to your ad in the February 1 *Sunday Times*."

▶ "I am interested in obtaining an entry-level paralegal position with your firm."

▶ "We met last July at the NALA Convention. I will be graduating from my paralegal program in May."

The first paragraph also usually indicates that your resume is enclosed for consideration, although this may also be in the closing paragraph.

In the body of the letter, you want to explain why your training and experience make you the right person for the job. Highlight and summarize the information in your resume, and take advantage of the opportunity to include more about yourself and your skills. For example, life experience that can't be easily incorporated into a resume can smoothly find its way into your cover letter. For example, instead of writing, "Before paralegal school, I worked at The Store for two years, and before that at The Shop for three years," try something like, "I have five years of retail experience during which I interacted with the public on a daily basis." The body of the letter is your opportunity to explain why the employer should care about your experience and training.

In the body of the letter you can also include information about how soon you are available for employment or why (if it's the case) you are applying for a job out of town. You may also include things that you are looking for in a job—if they are either non-negotiable or are flattering to the employer. Make a direct reference to the specific position and organization. Here are some examples:

▶ "I will graduate on May 16 and will be available for employment immediately. A position with your firm appeals to me because I understand you do a great deal of plaintiff employment work, and this is a field in which I am very interested. Employment law was one of the electives I chose as a student. In addition, at this time I am looking for part-time employment and I believe you currently have a part-time opening."

▶ "Although my internship was with the County Attorney's Office, I have come to realize that while that work was intensely interesting, I would prefer a position in the private sector that will afford me the opportunity to call on my real estate experience and my paralegal training. I believe your firm is the place for me and I am certain I would be an asset to you."

▶ "As you look at my resume, you will notice that although I am just now finishing my paralegal training, I offer a background in administration and problem solving. Since your company has recently undergone a major expansion, I believe you would find me a valuable addition to your staff."

Finally, the last paragraph (some people prefer it to be two short paragraphs) should thank the recipient of the letter, make a reference to future contact, and offer to provide further information. Examples of effective closing paragraphs include:

▶ "Thank you for your consideration. Please contact me at the address or phone number above if you need any further information."
▶ "I look forward to meeting you to discuss this job opening."
▶ "Thank you and I look forward to speaking with you in person."
▶ "I would welcome the opportunity to discuss the match between my skills and your needs in more detail. You can contact me at the address or phone number above, except for the week of the 27th, when I will be out of town. Thank you for your time."

INTERVIEWING SUCCESSFULLY

The last step in the job search process, and the one that causes the most anxiety among job seekers, is the interview. A face-to-face meeting with your potential employer gives him or her the chance to decide if you are the right person for the job, and you the chance to decide if the job is right for you. While it is normal to be nervous during an interview, there are many things you can do to calm your fears. The most worthwhile thing you can do is gain a solid understanding of the interview process, and your role in it. By carefully reading the following information, and following the suggestions made, you will greatly improve your chances for interviewing success.

Be Prepared

Research your potential employer before your interview and be ready to demonstrate your knowledge. Learn about the type of law practiced in the firm, or the business of a corporation or non-profit. If you're interviewing with a government agency, gain an understanding of its workings. The section of this book entitled "Researching the Field" explained many ways to get the information you're looking for. If you've already done your homework, be sure to refamiliarize yourself just before an interview. If not, now is the time to get the research done.

Preparation should also include practice—find someone to act as an interviewer, and have him or her take you through a mock interview. Ask for an honest evaluation of your performance, and work on those areas your "interviewer" feels you can improve.

Act Professionally

Take the interviewing process very seriously. You are entering the professional world, and you want to show that you fit into that environment. Make several extra copies of your resume, letters of recommendation, and your list of references to bring to your interview. You will also want to bring your daily planner, along with your research materials, a pad, and a working pen. All of this paperwork will fit nicely in a briefcase or portfolio. On your pad, write down the company's name, interviewer's name, address, telephone number, and directions to the location of the interview.

It's very important to be on time for your interview. Allow extra time for traffic and getting lost if the interview is in an unfamiliar location. Schedule your travel time so that you are in the lobby 10 minutes before your interview starts. This will give you time to relax before you begin.

Your appearance is the very first thing a potential employer will notice when you arrive for an interview, so make a positive first impression. Be sure that your clothes are free of stains and wrinkles, and your shoes are shined. If you must make a choice, it is better to be overdressed than underdressed. Personal hygiene is also critical; your hair should be neat, and fingernails clean.

On the morning of your interview, read a local newspaper and watch a morning news program so you're aware of the day's news events and will be able to discuss them with the interviewer. Many interviewers like to start off an interview with small talk. You want to appear knowledgeable about what's happening in the world around you.

Speak Confidently

Greet your interviewer with a firm handshake and an enthusiastic smile. Speak with confidence throughout your interview and let your answers convey your assumption that you will be offered the job. For example, phrase your questions this way: "What would my typical day consist of?" "How many paralegals work here, and what are their areas of expertise?" Answer questions in complete sentences; however, don't ramble on too long in answering any one question. Many hiring managers will ask questions that don't have a right or wrong answer; they ask such questions to evaluate your problem-solving skills.

Keep in mind that a potential employer is not allowed to ask you about your marital status, whether you have kids or plan to, your age, your religion, or your race (these kinds of questions may be asked on anonymous affirmative action forms). If you are asked such a question, you can say, "It's illegal for you to ask me that" and then sit silently until the interviewer says something. Or you can say something like, "I don't understand the question; what it is you want to know?" Better yet, figure out why they are asking the question, and address that issue. Then, the answer to "Do you have children?" becomes "If you're asking if I can travel and work overtime, that's generally not a problem."

Below are listed some general guidelines to follow when answering questions in an interview:

▶ Use complete sentences and proper English.
▶ Don't be evasive, especially if you're asked about negative aspects of your employment history.
▶ Never imply that a question is "stupid."
▶ Don't lie or stretch the truth.

▶ Be prepared to answer the same questions multiple times. Make sure your answers are consistent, and never reply, "You already asked me that."

▶ Never apologize for negative information regarding your past.

▶ Avoid talking down to an interviewer, or making them feel less intelligent than you are.

Ask Questions

You usually will be given the opportunity to ask the interviewer questions, so be prepared. Have a list of questions ready in advance. There's much you need to know about the firm to determine if it is a good fit for you. It's not a one-way street—while you are being evaluated, you are also evaluating the firm. If you don't ask any questions, the interviewer may think that you aren't interested in the position. Of course, you may ask about almost anything. You may want to know about the kinds of assignments you can expect, whether you will be able to follow cases from start to finish, whether you will have the opportunity to specialize, who manages paralegals and determines their assignments. These are all legitimate questions. You may also have questions about the resources of the firm, such as the computers and library. The number of billable hours you will be expected to produce is certainly something you will want to know.

If the firm is large, you can ask about its structure. For example, is there a paralegal department or are paralegals assigned to attorneys? Do paralegals have secretarial support? Is there a paralegal training program in place? If the firm is small, you may ask how long it has employed paralegals, whether it plans to hire more in the future, and whether paralegals are expected to do significant clerical work. In any size firm, you can ask about chances for promotion.

Anticipate the Questions You Will Be Asked

As part of your job interview preparation, think about the types of questions the interviewer will ask. Obviously, since you're applying for a job as a paralegal, you should anticipate detailed questions about the skills you possess and the experience you have using those skills.

Spend time developing well thought out, complete, and intelligent answers. Thinking about them, or even writing out answers on paper will be helpful, but what will benefit you the most is actual practice answering interview questions out loud. Stage a mock interview with someone you trust, who will evaluate your responses honestly.

Most of the questions you will be asked will be pretty obvious, but be prepared for an interviewer to ask you a few that are unexpected. By doing this, the interviewer will be able to see how you react and how well you think on your feet.

The following are common interview questions, along with suggestions on how you can best answer them:

- ▶ What can you tell me about yourself? (Stress your skills and accomplishments. Avoid talking about your family, hobbies, or topics not relevant to your ability to do the job.)
- ▶ Why have you chosen to pursue a career as a paralegal? (Give specific reasons and examples.)
- ▶ In your personal or professional life, what has been your greatest failure? What did you learn from that experience? (Be open and honest. Everyone has had some type of failure. Focus on what you learned from the experience and how it helped you to grow as a person.)
- ▶ Why did you leave your previous job? (Try to put a positive spin on your answer, especially if you were fired for negative reasons. Company downsizing, a company going out of business, or some other reason that was out of your control is a perfectly acceptable answer. Remember, your answer will probably be verified.)
- ▶ What would you consider to be your biggest accomplishments at your last job? (Talk about what made you a productive employee and valuable asset to your previous employer. Stress that teamwork was involved in achieving your success, and that you work well with others.)
- ▶ In college, you were a (insert subject) major. Why did you choose (insert subject) as your major? (Explain your interest in the subject matter, where that interest comes from, and how it relates to your current career-related goals.)

▶ What are your long-term goals? (Talk about how you have been following a career path, and where you think this pre-planned career path will take you in the future. Describe how you believe the job you're applying for is a logical step forward.)

▶ Why do you think you're the most qualified person to fill this job? (Focus on the positive things that set you apart from the competition. What's unique about you, your skill set and past experiences. What work-related experience you have that relates directly to this job.)

▶ What have you heard about this firm that is of interest to you? (Focus on the firm's reputation. Refer to positive publicity, personal recommendations from employees, or published information that caught your attention. This shows you've done your research.)

▶ What can you tell about yourself that isn't listed in your resume? (This is yet another opportunity for you to sell yourself to the employer. Take advantage of the opportunity.)

Avoiding Common Interview Mistakes

Once you get invited by a potential employer to come in for an interview, do everything within your power to prepare, and avoid the common mistakes often made by applicants. Remember that for every job you apply for, there are probably dozens of other paralegals who would like to land that same position.

The following are some of the most common mistakes applicants make while preparing for or participating in job interviews, with tips on how to avoid making these mistakes.

▶ Don't skip steps in your interview preparation. Just because you've been invited for an interview, you can't afford to "wing it" once you get there. Prior to the interview, spend time doing research about the company, its products/services and the people you will be meeting with.

▶ Never arrive late for an interview. Arriving even five minutes late for a job interview is equivalent to telling an employer you don't want the job. The day before the interview, drive to the interview location and determine exactly how to get there and how long it takes. On the day of the interview, plan on arriving at least ten minutes early and use the restroom before you begin the actual interview.

▶ Don't neglect your appearance. First impressions are crucial. Make sure your clothing is wrinkle-free and clean; that your hair is well groomed, and that your make-up (if applicable) looks professional. Always dress up for an interview, even if the dress code at the company is casual. Also, be sure to brush your teeth prior to an interview, especially if you've eaten recently.

▶ Prior to an interview, avoid drinking any beverages containing caffeine. Chances are, you will already be nervous about the interview. Drinking coffee or soda won't calm you down.

▶ Don't go into the interview unprepared. Prior to the interview, use your research to compile a list of intelligent questions to ask the employer. These questions can be about the company, its products/services, its methods of doing business, the responsibilities of the job you're applying for, and so on. When it's time for you to answer questions, always use complete sentences.

▶ Never bring up salary, benefits, or vacation time during the initial interview. Instead, focus on how you (with all of your skills, experience, and education) can become a valuable asset to the company you're interviewing with. Allow the employer to bring up the compensation package to be offered.

▶ Refrain from discussing your past earning history or what you're hoping to earn. An employer typically looks for the best possible employees for the lowest possible price. Let the employer make you an offer first. When asked, tell the interviewer you're looking for a salary/benefits package that's in line with what's standard in the industry for someone with your qualifications and experience. Try to avoid stating an actual dollar figure.

▶ During the interview, avoid personal topics. There are questions that an employer can't legally ask during an interview situation or on an employment application (as mentioned on page 151). In addition to these topics, refrain from discussing sex, religion, politics, and any other highly personal topics.

▶ Never insult the interviewer. It's common for an interviewer to ask what you might perceive to be a stupid or irrelevant question. In some cases, the interviewer is simply testing to see how you will respond. Some questions are asked to test your morals or determine your level of honesty. Other types of questions are used simply to see how you will react in a tough situation. Try to avoid getting caught up in trick questions. Never tell an interviewer their question is stupid or irrelevant.

▶ Throughout the interview, avoid allowing your body language to get out of control. For example, if you're someone who taps your foot when you're nervous, make sure you're aware of your habit so you can control it in an interview situation.

▶ If your job interview takes place over lunch or dinner, refrain from drinking alcohol of any kind.

Follow Up

It's a common belief that by conducting a job interview, the interviewer is simply doing his or her job, which is to fill the position(s) the employer has available. As a result of this belief, many job seekers show no gratitude to the interviewer. This is a mistake. Sending a personal and well-thought out note immediately after an interview will not only keep your name fresh in the hiring manager's mind, but will also show that you have good follow-up skills, and that you're genuinely interested in the job opportunity.

Individual and personalized thank-you notes should be sent out within 24 hours of your interview, to everyone you met with when visiting a potential employer. Send separate notes containing different messages to each person you met with, addressing each using the recipient's full name and title. Make sure you spell names correctly.

Thank-you notes may be typewritten on personal stationery, following a standard business letter format. A more personal alternative is to write your thank-you note on a professional looking note card, which can be purchased at any stationery, greeting card, or office supply store. The personal touch makes a positive impression and helps to separate you from your competition.

Keep your message brief and to the point. Thank the interviewer for taking the time out of his or her busy schedule to meet with you, and for considering you for the job opening available. Make sure you mention the exact paralegal position you applied for.

In one or two sentences, highlight the important details discussed in your interview. You want the interviewer to remember you. Don't mention issues under negotiation, such as salary, benefits, concerns, and work schedule. Finally, reaffirm your interest in the paralegal position and invite further contact with a closing sentence such as "I look forward to hearing from you soon."

Last Thoughts on Interviewing

There are two more important things to keep in mind while going through interviews. Both will help you to keep not only your interview, but the whole job search process, in perspective. The first is that even if you apply and interview for a job, you don't have to take it. The other is that good interviewers try to sell you on coming to work for them.

Understanding that you aren't required to take a job just because it's offered makes the interview seem less like a life-or-death situation and more like an opportunity to get to know at least one person at the hiring firm. You will feel a greater sense of confidence and ease when you keep this in mind. The paralegal position you're interviewing for isn't the only one available, so if it feels like a bad fit for you, or for them, move on.

Realizing that interviewers should be trying to sell you on coming to work for them is helpful too. A good interviewer has one goal in mind: finding a qualified person to fill the job opening. They already think you're a possibility, which is why you were invited to interview. Once you're there, it's the interviewer's job to convince you that you would be very happy working at his or her firm. Evaluate the information you're given about the work environment; does it fit with what you've seen and heard about the firm? Be attuned to the tactics of the interviewer.

Finally, there will be an end to the job search process. You will be offered a position that meets your wants and needs, and you will accept it. Chapter 6 details what happens after you begin work, helping you to maximize your potential for success in your new career.

THE INSIDE TRACK

Who: Manolo Murillo

What: Immigration Paralegal

Where: Los Angeles, California

INSIDER'S STORY

I was born in Bakersfield, California, shortly after my parents emigrated there from Mexico City. Growing up in a largely Hispanic community in southern California, the subjects of immigration and citizenship were often an issue among family and friends.

I had been working for a law firm as a paralegal for three years when I met an immigration lawyer who was starting his own law firm in my hometown, and he needed a legal assistant. I had often thought to myself exactly what he told me—our community lacked a really good lawyer to assist the hardworking people that desired citizenship. It seemed to me (and I viewed it firsthand when my father went through the naturalization process when I was a teen) that many of the so-called immigration specialists were more interested in taking advantage than actually helping out. After a short time assisting the lawyer, and helping out people from all over the world, it didn't take me long to realize that I made the right choice by entering into the immigration field.

I have been working as a paralegal for ten years law now, seven of them assisting in immigration law. Our firm's clients are usually Latin American or Mexican, and we often work pro bono—helping hardworking people like my parents is all the payment I need. On occasion, I will also conduct free information seminars at a local church.

Believe it or not, I originally became a paralegal because I wanted to make a lot of money. If I stayed with the big firm, I would be making much more than I am now. But I quickly learned that helping people out was much more rewarding than monetary gain. Working so closely with the lawyer and his clients made me want to be able to fully practice law, so I applied to law school, got accepted, and will be attending UCLA law school this coming fall. Being a paralegal opened up my eyes to my life's calling, and gave me invaluable experience for my future career as a lawyer.

CHAPTER six

SUCCEEDING ON THE JOB

IN THIS chapter, you will learn how to succeed once you've landed a job as a paralegal. You will find out how to fit into your new work environment, whether a law firm, nonprofit organization, or corporation employs you. Basics on forming positive relationships with the people you work with and managing your time effectively are also covered. Finally, a number of other ways in which you can put your career on the fast track, from finding a mentor to handling criticism professionally, will be examined.

CONGRATULATIONS! YOU'VE worked hard to get the paralegal training you need, and gone through the job search process. Now, you're employed in your first job as a legal assistant. Succeeding in your new position is your next goal. You have an understanding of a paralegal's basic duties and how to perform them, but your training didn't cover how to manage work relationships, or how to acclimate yourself to a new work environment. There is much to learn regarding how to perform well on the job, beyond what you were taught in the classroom. Many of these topics will be touched on, including finding a mentor and learning from one so that you will be armed with the knowledge you need to succeed.

FITTING INTO THE WORKPLACE CULTURE

As a paralegal, you may find employment with a law firm, a corporation, a government agency, a nonprofit, or a legal service organization. The workplace cultures of these employers vary greatly. Even among law firms you will find great differences; one may be formal and stiff, another is relaxed and casual, and yet another lies somewhere in between. Understanding the workplace culture of your employer will help you succeed in your new career by knowing what's expected of you, and what you can expect in return.

Despite going through many changes in the past several decades, law firms, for the most part, are still conservative and traditional. They expect their employees to bill a set number (or more) of hours, and that can mean a long work week. If a trial date is coming up, and everyone from partners to secretaries is preparing in the office until 11 P.M., you will be expected to do the same. You may notice that it's common practice to show up for a few hours on the weekend, either to complete an assignment, or to bring your billable hours up. Depending on the size of your firm, you may be asked to perform a wide or very small range of tasks. Larger firms tend to demand specialization, while smaller ones need everyone to be proficient in many areas of the law.

Until you're there for a while, you won't know all that the culture entails, but you will learn faster if you are in tune to it. Pay careful attention to the work habits of your coworkers, and follow suit. If everyone packs his or her own lunch and eats in the law library, do the same. If all of the women in the firm wear dresses or suits with skirts, don't try to start a trend by wearing pants. Similarly, if all the men leave their jackets and ties on all day, you should, too. After some time has passed, you will know better which customs and traditions you must follow and which you can deviate from.

If you go to work for the legal services/environmental law/nonprofit crowd, you will find a less conservative, more casual work culture. In offices like these, except on days when you go to court, jeans and T-shirts may be appropriate attire. These employers may prefer and even encourage individuals to be themselves, giving them a wide range of responsibilities and expecting them to work independently. They tend to leave tradition behind in pursuit of new and better ways to get the job done. Even so, there is an office environment that has its unwritten rules. As with employment at a law firm, you will need to pay careful attention in your first few weeks on the job. Do things similarly to the way the other paralegals do until you feel you've got a good working knowledge of the workplace culture.

Employment with a corporation offers yet another work environment for the paralegal. The tasks of an in-house legal department tend to be steadier and more predictable than they are in law firms. There is less of a chance that you will be stuck at work late into the night preparing for a trial. Your job may entail a very narrow range of responsibilities. Thus, your work week will probably be closer to 40 hours.

The corporate culture relies on a reporting structure and hierarchy to accomplish defined goals. Many large companies adopt this style simply because they have so many people to deal with. One manager (or president or vice president) cannot talk to everyone in the company all the time about their ideas. Instead, there's a functional reporting system. You might have a president, who has seven vice presidents, who has seven directors, who has seven managers, one of whom has you and several other paralegals in his or her reporting chain.

For employees, the advantage in this type of culture is usually security—job security, the availability of additional training (often company paid), and a good, long-term salary with stock options and other perquisites. The disadvantage is that employees do not have as much freedom as in other cultures, and may have to spend more time writing reports and filling out forms than do those in other workplace cultures. In a highly corporate culture, job titles are clearly defined, there is a pre-defined path to follow for raises and promotions, and there is little opportunity for an employee to shine outside of their own defined job.

You may find that after your first week on the job, you don't fit into the workplace culture of your employer. While first impressions are important, you should give yourself some time in your new position before deciding for certain that it isn't working. As we've mentioned above, it takes time to understand an office environment, and learn all of its unwritten rules. Give yourself a number of weeks or even months to fully integrate yourself into the culture of your new workplace.

MANAGING WORK RELATIONSHIPS

From the moment you began applying for jobs and participating in job interviews, you were establishing and building on your professional reputation. Your reputation may be defined as what people think of you in terms of your personality, competence, and attitude. This perception contributes greatly to what coworkers, subordinates, superiors, clients, and anyone else with whom you come into professional contact might say or think about you.

Your success as a paralegal will depend in large part on the business relationships you develop and cultivate. This refers to how you get along with others, particularly those you work with. Making a conscious effort to respect others, and becoming a "people person," and "team player" while on the job will help your career immensely.

Basic Rules

When it comes to building and maintaining professional relationships, some basic rules apply to any workplace.

Sometimes peace is better than justice

You may be absolutely, 100% sure you are right about a specific situation. Unfortunately, you may have coworkers who doubt you or who flatly disagree with you. This is a common occurrence in the workplace.

In some situations, you need to assert your position and convince the disbelievers to trust your judgment. Your previous track record and reputation will go a long way in helping to convince people to trust your opinions, ideas, and decisions. However, carefully consider the gravity of the situation before you stick your neck out.

In other words, in a work environment, choose your battles wisely. For instance, go ahead and argue your position if you can prevent a catastrophe. On the other hand, if you are having a debate about an issue of taste, opinion, or preference, you may want to leave the situation alone or accept the decisions of your superiors. Let your recommendation(s) be known, but do not argue your point relentlessly. Sometimes you will be right and people will not listen to you. Always be open to compromise and be willing to listen to and consider the options and ideas of others.

Don't burn bridges

If you are in a disagreement, if you are leaving one employment situation for another, or if a project is ending, always leave the work relationship on a good note. Keep in mind that your professional reputation will follow you throughout your career. It will take years to build a positive reputation, but only one mistake could destroy it.

When changing jobs, don't take the opportunity to vent negative thoughts and feelings before you leave. While it might make you feel good in the short term, it will have a detrimental, lasting effect on your career and on people's perception of you. Someone you insulted could become your boss someday or be in a position to help you down the line. The legal field is a close-knit community, and many people know one another, either in person or by reputation.

If you wind up acting unprofessionally toward someone, even if you don't ever have contact with that person again, he or she will have contact with many other people and possibly describe you as hard to work with or rude. Your work reputation is very important; don't tarnish it by burning your bridges.

When changing employment situations, do so in a professional manner. There are countless reasons why someone leaves one job to pursue a career with another firm, but to maintain a good reputation within the industry, it's important to act professionally when you actually quit. Getting into a fight with your boss, shouting, "I quit!" and then stomping out of the building forever is never the best way to handle things. Even if you think your boss is incompetent, in the heat of anger, never let your negative feelings cause you to act unprofessionally.

Instead, if you get into a major disagreement with your employer, don't make a decision to quit impulsively. Spend a few days thinking about your decision. If you decide it's time to move on, start looking for a new job before actually tendering your resignation with your current employer. As a general rule, even if you're not getting along with your boss or coworkers, it's never a good idea to quit your current job until you've lined up a new one.

Once you've actually landed that new job, be prepared to give your current employer the traditional two weeks notice. Arrange a private meeting with your boss or with the appropriate person within the company, and offer your resignation in-person, following it up in writing with a friendly and professional letter. Some people give notice and then use their accumulated vacation or sick days to avoid showing up for work. This is not appropriate behavior. Even if your new employer wants you to start work immediately, they will almost always understand that as a matter of loyalty and professional courtesy, it is necessary for you to stay with your current employer for those two weeks after giving your notice.

During those last two weeks on the job, offer to do whatever you can to maintain a positive relationship with your coworkers and boss, such as offering to train your replacement. Make your exit from the firm as smooth as possible. Purposely causing problems, stealing from the employer, or sabotaging business deals are all actions that are unethical and totally inappropriate. Some firms will request your immediate departure when you quit, and will cut off your computer access and escort you out of the building, especially if you're leaving on a negative note. Prior to quitting, try to determine how past coworkers were treated, so you will know what to expect.

As you actually leave the company for the last time, take with you only your personal belongings and nothing that is considered the company's property. Make a point to return directly to your boss your office keys and any company-owned equipment that was in your possession. If possible, for your protection, obtain a written memo stating that everything was returned promptly and in working order.

Keep your work and social lives separate

You were hired to do a job, not to meet new friends and potential dates. While it's important to be friendly and form positive relationships with the people you work with, you should understand the risks associated with becoming too close. Personal relationships can interfere with your job performance, and your job performance can weaken or destroy a relationship. Consider that you might be asked to rate a coworker's job performance, and the coworker happens to be your best friend. Unless your friend is perfect in every way, you will either have to compromise the rating you were asked to give, or your friendship. You may also find yourself in the position of having to take work direction from a buddy, or fire someone with whom you've become good friends. All of these challenges can be difficult.

The challenges associated with at-work romances, however, can lead to disaster. Imagine the above situations again, substituting a romantic partner for the friend. What was difficult before seems nearly impossible. Not only are you endangering your job performance and the relationship, but you may also set yourself up to lose your job. There are many firms and corporations that frown upon office romances, and some firms have strict policies against them. If your coworkers find out about your romance, depending upon where you work, you could end up looking for another job.

Lawyers

Most paralegals work directly for an attorney or attorneys. As your superior, the attorney assigns tasks and evaluates your performance, and you report directly to her or him. You may travel together during the discovery phase of a case, or work together in court during a trial. When you get along well with the attorney, your job is made easier, and much more pleasant. When you consider that more time is spent with coworkers than families, it's a relationship you want to make work.

Aside from doing your job to the very best of your abilities, the most important factor in making your relationships with attorneys work is respecting the hierarchy of the relationship. While there are many tasks within the legal field that can be performed completely by paralegals, most cannot. As a paralegal, you are in a support position, and the person you're supporting is the attorney. He or she is the only one who can practice law, despite the excellent training you've received. However, along with that knowledge, remember that even as a supporting player, you are still a professional, and should act and expect to be treated as such.

Most attorneys will respect you as a professional, and contribute to the success of your working relationship. However, there are some who believe paralegals shouldn't exist. Fortunately, the number of lawyers who feel that way is shrinking, if for no other reason than that paralegals have been around for a while and most attorneys have had a positive experience with at least one of them. If you do run into an anti-paralegal lawyer, the best way to handle the relationship is to perform your job at the highest level possible. It is also imperative that you never, ever, do anything that this individual can interpret as practicing law.

Try to work with the personalities of your coworkers, rather than against them. If an attorney doesn't want to acknowledge the need for your skills as a paralegal, listen to her complaints. Why does she feel this way? It may be because she has a fear that you will step over the line and practice law, giving bad advice to a client or illegally performing a task she should have done herself. You can show this attorney that you know the difference in your roles, and that you know that as a paralegal, you cannot and will not do anything that may be construed as practicing law. Or, it simply may be that she doesn't understand what paralegals do, and has no idea how to use your skills to her advantage. Perhaps you can bring to her attention some work you did for another attorney at the firm, or point out gently that you could relieve some of her work burden by performing some of the tasks for her. Think of her attitude as an overcome-able obstacle, rather than a brick wall.

Other Coworkers

Attorneys aren't the only people you will need to get along with in your new position. Depending upon where you're employed, you will work in an office with fellow paralegals, a paralegal manager, secretaries, investigators, and others. No matter how difficult some of these coworkers might be, maintaining a professional respect for them will allow everyone to be more productive and successful. You will also enhance your own reputation as someone who rises above the more unsavory aspects of office relations, and who can get along well with others.

The following are some fundamental rules for fostering positive working relationships with your peers:

▶ Don't gossip about your boss, your coworkers, or anyone else. Gossip hurts the person being talked about, will inevitably come back to haunt you, and also can make you look like you don't have enough to do.

▶ Foster sharing relationships instead of competitive relationships. If you read an interesting article in a law journal or paralegal publication, share the information with your coworkers. A group of people who help each other develop professionally will shine as a team and as individuals. On the other hand, if you jockey for position and compete over everything, you will miss out on what you could learn from your co-workers (and will have to live in a strained work environment).

▶ Don't become known as a "backstabber" who only looks out for his or her self. Especially when it comes time for employee evaluations or being considered for a raise or promotion, you want to be considered a hard working, sincere, honest, "team player" who does his/her best work in the interest of the company as a whole.

Your Boss

Because your boss has a great amount of power over your career, your relationship with him or her is probably the most important one at work. The first rule for getting along is to understand the management style used by your boss, and adjust your expectations to work within that style. For instance, your first boss might be a hands-on person and help you troubleshoot problems. She might want to talk to you at least once a day to hear about your activities. You need to understand that this boss wants to empower you through a mentoring/teaching style.

On the other hand, your boss might want you to call him only if you have a problem and simply submit a weekly status report on your projects. You need to understand that this boss wants to empower you through a hands-off style that lets you find your own solutions. Both bosses may be good managers; they simply have different styles. Understand the value of each style and get the most from it.

Keep the lines of communication open not only about your immediate tasks at hand, but also about your career goals. Your boss may be very open to and encouraging of your ambitions, and could help you in a number of ways. Advice from someone who is already achieving what you'd like to someday achieve can be invaluable. More tangibly, you might get to create projects and strategies with your boss that get you closer toward your goals. No matter what your future career goals are, make a plan, share it with your boss, and get a few steps closer to achieving it.

Having an occasional disagreement with a superior is normal, but if your life is being ruined by the actions of a mean or difficult boss, it's up to you to take action and find a solution that you can be happy with. If you're in a situation where you don't see eye-to-eye with your boss, you have several options. First, evaluate the problem. Do you disagree about how a relatively small problem that won't come up often should be handled? Or, do you have very different opinions about a major element of your work for him or her? If it's a minor situation, you're probably better off doing it the boss's way. If it's major, you can also do nothing, live with the situation, hope that it doesn't get worse, and not let your relationship with your boss impact you emotionally. Or, you can quit your job and seek employment elsewhere. Either of these might appear to be the easiest solution to a larger problem, but neither will lead to long-term career fulfillment.

Your first goal should be to alter your attitude and behavior, doing whatever it takes to develop a relationship with your boss that revolves around mutual respect. Remember that there may be others who have had problems getting along with your boss, and they may be watching with interest how you handle the situation. Finding a way to work together even though you disagree can earn you respect and enhance your professional reputation.

The Client Relationship

In a great many paralegal jobs, more of your time will be spent with clients than with coworkers. This direct contact can be one of the most rewarding aspects of your job, but it can also be one of the most stressful. Think about why people need the services of a lawyer in the first place. Often, it's because they are facing a crisis. They may have been arrested or threatened, are getting divorced, or are contemplating death. Clients in corporate law face crises involving things like hostile takeovers and product liability suits. They come to a law firm at a low point—they may be under great stress, and need to resolve their crises.

Dealing with such people in a professional capacity can be difficult; you will need to be supportive, but also find out from them how best you can help. Interviewing a client in a crisis can be stressful, and requires compassion as well as great communication skills. If you find this aspect of your job difficult, you may find help from others in your firm or in your field who are better at handling it.

You may also have to deal with clients who have little knowledge about what paralegals are and what they do. They may either not want to talk to you, feeling you are somehow a poor substitute for a lawyer, or they may pressure you for legal opinions. In the first instance, a professional demeanor on your part will go a long way toward gaining a reluctant client's confidence. You may sometimes have to say, "Your lawyer trusts me to handle this matter. Please give me a chance to show you that trust is justified." In the second instance, remember that engaging in the unauthorized practice of law could jeopardize your job and your career. Don't do it; explain that while it's not your place to give legal advice, you will bring the matter to the attorney's attention, and get the information the client is requesting. That doesn't mean you can never answer a question; of course you will and should exercise your independent judgment. Dealing with clients can be a time for you to let your skills shine. Be aware of the stresses and possible complications, and perform your job with the highest level of professionalism.

Sexual Harassment

Both men and women can be the victims of unwanted sexual advances, or other inappropriate sexual behavior from superiors or coworkers. This victimization violates our rights; we all deserve to be treated with respect and dignity. In the workplace, we are protected from inappropriate sexual behavior through sexual harassment legislation. While inappropriate behavior can range from a single rude comment to daily passes, and some of it is subjective (one person may laugh off what another finds intolerable), the courts generally define sexual harassment based on the way the recipient feels. In other words, if something is making you uncomfortable, it may be considered harassment, and it is within your rights to do something to stop it.

Depending on the situation, you may simply need to point out the behavior to the offending party, and explain that you do not appreciate it and won't accept it again. Other circumstances, however, may call for more serious measures. Most firms and corporations have policies about sexual harassment, which include the appropriate way in which to report it. It pays to find out what these policies are, and take action if necessary.

MANAGING YOUR TIME

Effective time management is crucial to the practice of law. There are all kinds of deadlines and dates that need to be met, and they need to be done so efficiently and thoroughly. Not having a system in place that keeps track of deadlines and tasks can mean disaster for you and your clients. Being able to know what needs to be done when, and having the work habits necessary for getting it all done well and on time are crucial to your success as a paralegal.

Daily Work Activities

Practicing good habits when dealing with your daily work activities is essential for all paralegals. You will be expected to perform a variety of tasks, many during the same time period. In order to keep things moving smoothly, and complete your assignments well and on time, remember the following:

1. **Know the requirements of your job and what your boss expects of you.** Define your role and know what you are expected to deliver on a daily basis.
2. **Don't get trapped by interruptions and time wasters.** Every job is subject to time wasters. Sometimes you may get caught up by people who want to chat, or you may fall into the trap of playing computer games or reading the news. It is important to allow yourself a small amount of relaxation throughout the day, but set limits for yourself—such as 15 minutes per day—so it doesn't get out of control. If you work with a social, chatty person, don't let yourself be distracted or interrupted. If you are working on something, let your coworker know that you are busy and can perhaps talk later, during lunch. If you do have time to talk to your coworker, try to steer the conversation to work-related topics. Use the time to learn something new from your coworker rather than just chat. And remember, you can only bill hours spent doing your work. The more time you waste, the more time you will spend in the office.

3. **Keep a day planner.** Identify one place where you write (or type) everything down, whether it is a daily planner, personal digital assistant (PDA), or specialized scheduling software for your computer. This is the number one "secret" of those who get nearly everything on their to-do list done, when it needs to be done. It's not that these people have better memories than yours; they are just better organized, and can find the information they need at a glance, because they keep it all in one place.

Improving Time Management Skills

If you find that this is an area in which you could improve, begin to do so immediately. Learning time management skills won't add more hours to the work day, but it will allow you to use all of your time more productively, reduce the stress in your life, better focus on what's important, and ultimately, get more done. If you've decided to use a time management tool such as a computer program or personal digital assistant, spend the time necessary to learn how to use it properly. These tools are only as effective as their user, and although it may take a large time investment to get started, it will be well worth it.

Next, over the course of several days, analyze how you spend every minute of your day. Determine what takes up the majority of your time, but diminishes your productivity. Perhaps you experience countless interruptions from coworkers, long telephone calls, you don't have well-defined priorities, your work area is messy and disorganized, you have too much to do and become overwhelmed, or you're constantly forced to participate in unscheduled meetings. As you examine how you spend your day, pinpoint the biggest time wasters that are keeping your from getting your most important work done.

Take major projects, goals, and objectives and divide them into smaller, more manageable tasks. You will need to incorporate your to-do list into your daily planner, allowing you to schedule your time. Make sure you attempt to complete your high-priority items and tasks early in the day, giving those items your full attention. Also, make sure you list all of your pre-scheduled appointments in your daily schedule, allowing ample time to get to and from the appointments, and if necessary, prepare for them in advance.

Once you commit to using a time management tool, it's important to remain disciplined, using it continuously until it becomes second nature. Initially, you may have to spend up to 30 minutes per day planning your time and creating your to-do list, but ultimately, you will begin saving up to several hours per day. Learning to better manage your time will boost your productivity, which will ultimately make you more valuable to an employer, putting you in a better position to receive a raise or promotion.

Calendaring

Almost every task performed by a paralegal has a deadline. The courts have rules about when documents such as interrogatories and responses to complaints must be filed. Trial and hearing dates are set by the court and must be strictly adhered to. In addition to courts, government agencies also determine when certain documents need to be filed.

The practice of keeping track of deadlines and which tasks have been completed or need completing is known as "calendaring." As you might imagine, of all the work lawyers want to give up to paralegals, calendaring is at the top of the list. It will be up to you to let your boss know that something is due to be filed, or an important court date is impending. If you're already using a time management tool effectively for daily work activities, it won't be difficult to perform your calendaring duties with ease.

Before the advent of computer programs and PDAs, paralegals and legal secretaries used "ticklers" to organize their time and keep track of deadlines. Ticklers were often nothing more than recipe boxes with 3 x 5 cards and a divider for every day of the month. When a new project began, several cards would be used to track it. One might read "X v Y appeal brief due one month from today." If the final brief was due on January 4, that card would be filed under December 7. Then, on December 21, the card would read "X v Y appeal brief due two weeks from today," and so on. As the work progressed, other cards would be added as a reminder of what was done and what was left; for example, the card for a certain day might read, "complete standing research and check on statute of limitations." Thus the tickler made sure there were no surprise due dates.

Today, technology makes it much easier to create a tickler. But, as mentioned above, a time management tool is only as good as the person who's using it. It's your responsibility to be sure that all pertinent information, as well as every important date, be included. A computer program doesn't know you have a response due next week unless you tell it so. Make sure you come up with a surefire method for doing your part of the calendaring.

Juggling Multiple Tasks

Remember that most of a law office's schedule is determined by someone else. Then remember that you will probably be working for more than one attorney. Now picture several attorneys handing you projects that take three days to complete, and are all due tomorrow. Relax. There are a number of ways to handle this situation. First, just because somebody says something is due tomorrow doesn't mean it really is. You may find yourself working for someone who says "I need this right away!" about every project he hands you. After a short time on the job, you should be able to determine who likes to exaggerate and create time-crunch tension, and who really needs your help right away.

Second, no matter how much you want to please your bosses, you can't take on more than one three-day project and have them all done tomorrow (whether you can do even one is questionable as well). Appeal to the lawyer who knows that three three-day projects can't be completed in 24 hours. You're not going to be fired if you say, "I can't do that" to the second and third requests. Third, just because someone asked you first doesn't mean that person's task is more urgent.

The key elements of organization are communication and knowledge. Find out as much as you can about each assignment, and keep your bosses informed about your progress. Figure out which project really has to be done tomorrow and which can wait or be done by someone else. Then, when one attorney says, "You have to do this first! It's due next week!" you can say, "Yes, but this is due tomorrow." Don't allow yourself to get flustered by the lawyers who always seem to operate in "crisis mode." And remember, you're only human. Even if you pulled an all-nighter, you alone could not complete three three-day projects by tomorrow!

Time for You

When you're at work every day all week long, it becomes difficult to get your *life tasks* done. When you have a family, and you're juggling the needs and schedules of a number of people, it can be even more difficult. Just as with your job, the key to getting everything done (with time to spare to relax!) is organization. Below are some tips to help you integrate your job with your life.

▶ Make "to-do" lists and prioritize the tasks you need to accomplish. Keep a list of things you need to do, buy, return, pick up, and drop off, using the same time management tool employed at work (unless it's a computer program). A day planner or PDA works best. Organize your list according to places you will stop. Keep grocery items on one list, pharmacy items on another, dry cleaning on a third, and so on. Cross things off the lists when you have finished them so you can see what you have to do at a glance.

▶ Use your lunch hour to run errands at least once a week. Identify resources that are close to your work for things you can do during your lunch hour—doctor, dentist, dry cleaner, shoe repair, car repair, hardware store, and so on.

▶ Use the commute between home and work to take care of life's other necessities, such as stopping in at the supermarket after picking up the kids at daycare.

MENTORS

Finding and learning from a mentor can be an essential element in your success. It's probably one of the best ways to continue your education on the job, giving you the kind of insider information not covered during your training. Mentoring can also provide you with a professional "coach"—someone who sees your job performance and knows ways in which you can improve upon it. A mentor is someone you identify as successful, and with whom you create an informal teacher–student relationship. Enter into the relationship intending to observe your mentor carefully, learning from him or her as much as possible.

Finding a Mentor

You will probably need to actively search for a mentor, unless someone decides to take you under his or her wing and show you the ropes. A mentor can be anyone from a senior paralegal to an attorney or legal department head. There is no formula for who makes a good mentor; it is not based on title, level of seniority, or years in the field. Instead, the qualities of a good mentor are based on a combination of willingness to be a mentor, level of expertise in a certain area, teaching ability, and attitude.

When looking for a mentor, keep in mind the following questions:

▶ Who in your firm has a great reputation as a true professional?
▶ Does the potential mentor tackle problems in a reasonable manner until they are resolved?
▶ What is it that people admire about the potential mentor? Do the admirable qualities coincide with your values and goals?
▶ Is he or she strong in areas that you are weak?

When you think you've found someone to be your mentor, spend some time watching that person on the job. You can learn a lot about him or her through observation. When asked a question, does she take the time to help you find the solution, or does she point you toward someone else who can help you? The one who takes the time to help you resolve your question is the better choice for a mentor. Observe your potential mentor when he is working on a problem. Does he do so in a calm manner? Does the problem get resolved? If so, you may have found a good mentor.

Also spend time listening to what others have to say about your potential mentor. Professional reputations can help you to narrow down your search. If you have difficulty interviewing stressed-out clients, find someone who's known for putting people at ease while getting their job done. If your legal research skills are weak, discover who the paralegal is that every attorney seems to go to with a research question.

Learning From a Mentor

Once you've entered into a mentoring relationship, intend to learn all you can. While there are no set rules about what a mentor can teach you, there are some specifics that are part of the "curriculum" in many mentoring relationships. The following is a list of things you may learn from a mentor:

▶ Client interaction skills
▶ What to expect in the legal work environment
▶ How to communicate with the chain of command in your firm
▶ In-depth knowledge about the technology used by your firm
▶ The best paralegal magazines, websites, and other resource material
▶ What conferences/classes/training programs you should attend

Once you find someone who seems to be the ideal mentor, don't feel compelled to stick with him or her forever. Career growth may open up new possibilities to you in new areas of specialization. If that happens, you will probably want to find additional mentors who can show you the ropes in the new environment. However, any former mentors you can keep as friends may not only help you career-wise, but they can also enrich your life in personal ways.

PROMOTING YOURSELF

There are a number of other things you can do to keep your career moving in a positive direction. You can't wait for opportunities to land in your lap; rather, you need to be proactive by promoting yourself. Then, you will create opportunity for yourself. Day-to-day, you will have the chance to get the interesting work assignments, or be satisfied doing similar tasks over and over. Keeping track of what you do and when you do it will create a permanent record of your accomplishments—something you will want to have as verification if your work is ever called into question, or remembered incorrectly. Finally, by handling any criticism professionally, remaining calm, listening to what is said, and offering to make changes, you will come out on top even in the stickiest of situations. Next, we'll discuss these ways of promoting yourself in greater detail.

Taking Control of Your Assignments

You may find yourself working for an attorney or attorneys who still aren't sure what a paralegal can do. They might, out of ignorance, assume that you can only do a very limited number of things, such as research. So, you are given an assignment to do some research, you do a good job, and your next assignment is to do more research. After a while, you realize that's all you ever do. Every time this attorney gives you a research assignment, don't think to yourself about the many other skills you have that are not being utilized. Instead, offer something concrete, such as, "after I finish, I can draft the complaint for you. I can have that done by next Thursday." Most attorneys are busy enough that they will be willing to let you try something new.

In addition, keep your ears open for the lawyers you work for to complain about how busy they are. You may hear, "I have a telephone hearing at 11:00 and a deposition this afternoon, and I have to finish an answer to a complaint by the filing deadline tomorrow!" A great response would be, "I can draft the answer for you and have it first thing in the morning. You can see if there need to be any changes, and then I can file it before end of business tomorrow." By volunteering to help with the workload, you also gain more responsibility and a chance to show off your writing skills.

Building on Your Reputation

No matter how well you work with others and how organized you are, in the end you will be judged by the product you put out. You want to develop a reputation as someone who gets an assignment, does it right, and does it on time. To accomplish this, whenever someone gives you a task, make sure you know exactly what is expected of you. When an attorney tells you to do research for a memo, ask him or her if you are to draft the memo, or whether the research should be organized in a particular way. And when the attorney tells you the research is needed "next week," find out if there is an appointment with the client and whether it is on Monday or Friday. If you don't have this kind of information, you may manage to do the assignment, but the attorney may be disappointed in the end result. It never hurts to get things in writing, either.

Keeping a Record of Your Work

As your career progresses, find a way to keep track of the work you do. This doesn't mean making unauthorized copies of documents to store in your own file; that could lead to breaches in client confidentiality. Simply keep a record of the work you do. On your calendar or elsewhere, write down when assignments were given, a brief description of the assignments, when and if they were modified, and when you completed them. That way, when your performance is reviewed and an attorney says, "I think you were late on the X research last month," you can look at your records and point out that you were told to put that work aside when another, more pressing, matter came up. It also allows you to chart, both for yourself and your bosses, the path your career has taken at the firm.

Some larger firms use forms for requesting in-house paralegal services. The information on these forms and their degree of detail varies a great deal, but in essence, their purpose is to outline the tasks required of the paralegal department. When you are the only paralegal working on a case, that request form will be given to you; when several paralegals will work on the case, each will be given a copy indicating which tasks are assigned to which person. If you keep a file with copies of these request forms—and make any notes on them about verbal instructions you received—you will be well on your way to having a complete record of the work you've done. When you do receive criticism about your job performance, you need to do three things. The first is to remain calm. You need to hear what is being said, and that is nearly impossible when you're upset. Listen and understand what is being said without trying to defend yourself or correcting the person who's critiquing your work.

Second, ask for clarification and concrete help to rectify the situation. If you've been told that you need to work on your writing skills, find out exactly what the problem is. If it's spelling and grammar, you can remedy the situation fairly easily by using the checks in your word processing software, and consulting dictionaries and grammar textbooks. If it's your writing style, find out how you can improve. One of the best ways to do this is to ask for writing samples that are considered to be excellent. On your next assignment, follow the sample as closely as possible in form and tone.

Third, follow any advice given, and ask the person who's critiquing you for help in the future. See if you can find a time when he or she can go over your brief and make specific suggestions for changes. The attorney may also be willing to read some early drafts in the future and give you feedback. By keeping calm, and responding in a non-defensive, professional manner, you can turn a negative critique into an opportunity for positive growth and change.

FINAL THOUGHTS

Litigation paralegal Gayle Lund says she highly recommends the paralegal profession, especially to young professionals starting out in their work life. "There's really a wide variety of opportunities in the field, especially for young people who can put in the time to network, to work a little bit of overtime, to get on the exciting projects, and to do some volunteer work. I think it's a great field, and I think it has a big future."

As we've noted throughout this book, the paralegal profession is growing, and it doesn't look likely to slow down anytime soon. Not only are there more paralegals working in the field, but paralegals also are moving in many new directions. The paralegal career pays quite well, is well respected, and affords you opportunities for advancement.

Probably the best thing about working in the legal profession, no matter what area you're in and no matter how routine your work may be, is that every once in a while you make a huge difference in someone's life. You might work toward a positive result in an area such as tobacco or breast-implant litigation, whose outcome affects thousands of people. Or, you might score a smaller victory, such as getting a used car dealer to take back a lemon and refund the money, getting a sign-language interpreter for a deaf student, or preventing the hostile takeover of a small corporation. These victories may affect just one person, but to him or her, they mean everything. You're not only doing work you enjoy, and getting the financial rewards for it, but you may be positively impacting the world around you.

THE INSIDE TRACK

Who: Cindy Lopez

What: President and Founder, NJParalegal.com,

                Paralegal Career Consultant

Where: New Jersey

INSIDER'S STORY

I knew the legal profession was where I was meant to be while I was attending Brookdale Community College in New Jersey two nights a week, and working full-time at a law office toward my AAS degree in Paralegal Studies.

When I graduated and received my degree, I did an internship, and used temp agencies for employment; I recommend both to any student or new paralegal. The internship gave me great insight into the inner workings of a law office. The temp positions helped me see what type of law I preferred, and gave me the experience of working in large, medium, and small firms, giving me the opportunity to decide in what setting I would ultimately prefer to work. For me, I realized that I preferred working for a small firm, or even a sole practitioner—the office is usually less strict and it is often like a family environment. It's a great situation because in those types of settings you have the ability to develop a good relationship with your boss, and access his or her expertise and professional knowledge. And if they gain confidence in you, they will often be more willing to give you more challenging work and responsibilities. Something else that I did, and I recommend to do, was join my college's Paralegal Alumni Association; it served me as an important resource, and a foundation for networking.

I love being a paralegal, but over the years I definitely encountered some challenges. When I started out, I did not realize that where you are located has a direct influence upon many things in the profession. For example, in New York's tri-state area, the closer to New York City you go, the better the salary, the positions, etc. However, where I'm based in central to southern New Jersey, paralegals are rarely hired or recognized as having a "profession" at all. Most of the employers in the area hire legal secretaries for clerical work and recent law school graduates for research, drafting of pleadings, and so on; even in the larger firms, it is difficult to get the title of "paralegal." I quickly realized the need for paralegals to network and to push for recognition. That's when I came up with the idea for NJParalegal.com. I envisioned it as an online community for paralegals to find jobs, schools, associations, career tips, newsletters, support, sharing, and more. And that is what it is has become.

I strived for change through legal community involvement and education. I became a member of the Legal Assistants' Association of New Jersey (LAANJ), the New Jersey State Bar Association, and my local chamber of commerce. My mission was dedicated to the support and recognition of the paralegal profession in New Jersey.

My advice for new or prospective paralegals is simple: Know what you are getting yourself into. As a paralegal you will hardly ever be bored or twiddling your thumbs. It is a fast paced profession with plenty of deadlines. Some people love that kind of environment, some people can't stand it—you have to realize what type of person you are. Also, as a paralegal you will be expected to know three things: 1) the legal process and rules, 2) the documents, and 3) your clients. As in any career, you will find the work rewarding and challenging if you truly like what you are doing. And, if your belief system coincides with your area of law, you will find this is also a field where there is opportunity to "make a difference" in the lives of others!

Appendix A

Professional Associations

In addition to contact information for national organizations and state bar associations, this appendix lists the affiliated organizations of the National Federation of Paralegal Associations. You'll also find a state-by-state listing of higher education agencies.

NATIONAL ORGANIZATIONS

The organizations listed below represent more than 30,000 paralegals, 500 paralegal managers, and 300 paralegal programs across the country.

Association for Paralegal Education
2965 Flowers Road South, Suite 105
Atlanta, GA 30341
Tel: 770-452-9877
Fax: 770-458-3314
E-mail: info@aafpe.org
www.aafpe.org

American Bar Association
Standing Committee on Legal Assistants
541 North Fairbanks Court, Mail Stop 15.1,
Chicago, IL 60611
Tel: 312-988-5617
Fax: 312-988-5483
E-mail:mbarmash@staff.abanet.org/legalassts
www.abanet.org

Association of Legal Administrators
175 East Hawthorn Parkway
Suite 325
Vernon Hills, IL 60061-1428
Tel: 847-816-1212
Fax: 847-816-1213
www.alanet.org

Legal Assistant Management Association
2965 Flowers Road South, Suite 105
Atlanta, GA 30341
Tel: 770-457-7746
Fax: 770-458-3314
E-mail: lamaoffice@aol.com
www.lamanet.org

National Association of Legal Assistants
1516 South Boston Avenue, Suite 200
Tulsa, OK 74119
Tel: 918-587-6828
Fax: 918-582-6772
E-mail: nalanet@nala.org
www.nala.org

National Federation of Paralegal
   Associations (NFPA)
P.O. Box 33108
Kansas City, MO 64114
Tel: 816-941-4000
Fax: 816-941-2725
E-mail: info@paralegals.org
www.paralegals.org

STATE BAR ASSOCIATIONS

Alabama Bar Association
415 Dexter Avenue
P.O. Box 671
Montgomery, AL 36104
Tel: 334-269-1515
Fax: 334-261-6310
www.alabar.org

Alaska Bar Association
507 L Street, Suite 602
Anchorage, AK 99501
Tel: 907-272-7469
Fax: 907-272-2932
E-mail: info@alaskabar.org
www.alaskabar.org

State Bar of Arizona
111 West Monroe, Suite 1800
Phoenix, AZ 85003
Tel: 602-252-4804
Fax: 602-271-4930
www.azbar.org

Arkansas Bar Association
400 West Markham
Little Rock, AR 72201
Tel: 507-375-4606
E-mail: arkbar1@swbell.net
www.arkbar.com

State Bar of California
180 Howard Street
San Francisco, CA 94105
Tel: 415-538-2000
www.calbar.org

Colorado Bar Association
1900 Grant Street, 9th Floor
Denver, CO 80203
Tel: 303-860-1115
Fax: 303-894-0821
www.cobar.org

Connecticut Bar Association
30 Bank Street
P.O. Box 350
New Britain, CT 06050
Tel: 860-223-4400
Fax: 860-223-4488
www.ctbar.org

Delaware State Bar Association
301 North Market Street
Wilmington, DE 19801
Tel: 302-658-5279
Fax: 302-658-5212
www.dsba.org

Bar Association of D.C.
1819 H Street NW, 12th Floor
Washington, DC 20006
Tel: 202-223-6600
Fax: 202-293-3388
E-mail: BAofDC@aol.com
www.badc.org

The Florida Bar
650 Apalachee Parkway
Tallahassee, FL 32399
Tel: 850-561-5600
Fax: 850-561-5826
www.flabar.org

State Bar of Georgia
800 The Hurt Building
50 Hurt Plaza
Atlanta, GA 30303
Tel: 404-527-8700
www.gabar.org

Hawaii State Bar Association
1132 Bishop Street, Suite 906
Honolulu, HI 96813
Tel: 808-537-1868
Fax: 808-521-7936
www.hsba.org

Idaho State Bar Association
P.O. Box 895
Boise, ID 83701
Tel: 208-334-4500
Fax: 208-334-4515
www2.state.id.us/isb

Illinois State Bar Association
Illinois Bar Center
424 South 2nd Street
Springfield, IL 62701
Tel: 217-525-1760
Fax: 217-525-0712
www.illinoisbar.org

Indiana State Bar Association
Indiana Bar Center
230 East Ohio Street, 4th Floor
Indianapolis, IN 46204
Tel: 317-639-5465
Fax: 317-266-2588
E-mail: isbaadmin@inbar.org
www.state.in.us/isba

Iowa State Bar Association
521 East Locust Street, Floor 3
Des Moines, IA 50309
Tel: 515-243-3179
www.iowabar.org/main.nsf

Kansas Bar Association
1200 South West Harrison Street
Topeka, KS 66612
Tel: 785-234-5696
Fax: 785-234-3813
www.ksbar.org

Kentucky Bar Association
514 West Main Street
Frankfort, KY 40601
Tel: 502-564-3795
Fax: 502-564-3225
www.kybar.org

Louisiana State Bar Association
601 Saint Charles Avenue
New Orleans, LA 70130
Tel: 504-566-1600
E-mail: lsbainfo@lsba.org
www.lsba.org

Maine State Bar Association
124 State Street
P.O. Box 788
Augusta, ME 04332
Tel: 207-622-7523
www.mainebar.org

Maryland State Bar Association, Inc.
520 West Fayette Street
Baltimore, MD 21201
Tel: 410-685-7878
Fax: 410-685-1016
E-mail: msba@msba.org
www.msba.org

Massachusetts Bar Association
20 West Street
Boston, MA 02111-1218
Tel: 617-338-0530
www.massbar.org

State Bar of Michigan
The Michael Franck Building
306 Townsend Street
Lansing, MI 48933
Tel: 517-346-6300
Fax: 517-482-6248
www.michbar.org

Minnesota State Bar Association
600 Nicollet Mall, #380
Minneapolis, MN 55402
Tel: 612-333-1183
www.mnbar.org

The Mississippi Bar
P.O. Box 2168
Jackson, MS 39225
Tel: 601-948-4471
Fax: 601-355-8635
www.msbar.org

The Missouri Bar
P.O. Box 119
Jefferson City, MO 65102
Tel: 573-635-4128
Fax: 573-835-2811
www.mobar.org

State Bar of Montana
46 Last Chance Gulch, #2A
P.O. Box 577
Helena, MT 59624
Tel: 406-442-7660
Fax: 406-442-7763
E-mail: mailbox@montanabar.org
www.montanabar.org

Nebraska State Bar Association
635 South 14th Street
P.O. Box 81809
Lincoln, NE 68501
Tel: 402-475-7091
www.nebar.com

The Nevada State Bar
600 East Charleston Boulevard
Las Vegas, NV 89104
Tel: 702-382-2200
Fax: 702-385-2878
www.nvbar.org

New Hampshire Bar Association
112 Pleasant Street
Concord, NH 03301
Tel: 603-224-6942
Fax: 603-224-2910
E-mail: NHBAinfo@nhbar.org
www.nhbar.org

New Jersey State Bar Foundation
New Jersey Law Center
1 Constitution Square
New Brunswick, NJ 08901
Tel: 732-249-5000
Fax: 732-828-0034
www.njsbf.org

State Bar of New Mexico
P.O. Box 25883
Albuquerque, NM 87125
Tel: 505-797-6000
Fax: 505-828-3765
www.nmbar.org

New York State Bar Association
1 Elk Street
Albany, NY 12207
Tel: 518-463-3200
www.nysba.org

North Carolina Bar Association
P.O. Box 3688
Cary, NC 27519
Tel: 919-677-0561
Fax: 919-677-0761
www.barlinc.org

State Bar Association of North Dakota
515 East Broadway, Suite 101
P.O. Box 2136
Bismarck, ND 58502
Tel: 701-255-1404
Fax: 701-224-1621
www.sband.org

Ohio State Bar Association
P.O. Box 16562
Columbus, OH 43216
Tel: 614-487-2050
Fax: 614-487-1008
E-mail: osba@ohiobar.org
www.ohiobar.org

Oklahoma Bar Association
1901 North Lincoln Blvd
P.O. Box 53036
Oklahoma City, OK 73152
Tel: 405-416-7000
Fax: 405-416-7001
www.okbar.org

Oregon State Bar
5200 Southwest Meadows Road
Lake Oswego, OR 97035
Tel: 503-620-0222
www.osbar.org

Pennsylvania Bar Association
100 South Street
P.O. Box 186
Harrisburg, PA 17108
Tel: 717-238-6715
Fax: 717-238-1204
E-mail: info@pabar.org
www.pabar.org

Rhode Island Bar Association
115 Cedar Street
Providence, RI 02903
Tel: 401-421-5740
Fax: 401-421-2703
E-mail: riba@ids.net
www.ribar.com

South Carolina Bar Association
950 Taylor Street
Columbia, SC 29202
Tel: 803-799-6653
Fax: 803-799-4118
www.scbar.org

State Bar of South Dakota
222 East Capitol Avenue
Pierre, SD 57501
Tel: 605-224-7554
www.sdbar.org

Tennessee Bar Association
221 4th Avenue N., Suite 400
Nashville, TN 37219
Tel: 615-383-7421
Fax: 615-297-8058
www.tba.org

State Bar of Texas
1414 Colorado Street, Suite 501
Austin, TX 78701
Tel: 512-463-1463
Fax: 512-463-1475
www.texasbar.org

Utah State Bar
645 South 200 East
Salt Lake City, UT 84111
Tel: 801-531-9077
Fax: 801-531-0660
www.utahbar.org

Vermont Bar Association
35–37 Court Street
P.O. Box 100
Montpelier, VT 05601
Tel: 802-223-2020
Fax: 802-223-1573
www.vtbar.org

Virginia State Bar
707 East Main Street, Suite 1500
Richmond, VA 23219
Tel: 804-775-0500
www.vsb.org

Washington State Bar Association
2101 Fourth Avenue, 4th Floor
Seattle, WA 98121
Tel: 206-443-WSBA
Fax: 206-727-8320
E-mail: questions@wsba.org
www.wsba.org

West Virginia State Bar
2006 Kanawha Boulevard East
Charleston, WV 25311
Tel: 304-558-2456
Fax: 304-558-2467
www.wvbar.org

State Bar of Wisconsin
P.O. Box 7158
Madison, WI 53707
Tel: 608-257-3838; 800-444-9404
Fax: 608-257-5502
www.wisbar.org

Wyoming State Bar
500 Randall Avenue
Cheyenne, WY 82001
Tel: 307-632-9061
E-mail: info@wyomingbar.org
www.wyomingbar.org

NFPA-AFFILIATED ORGANIZATIONS

ALABAMA

Gulf Coast Paralegal Association

P.O. Box 66705

Mobile, AL 36660

ALASKA

Alaska Association of Legal Assistants

P.O. Box 101956

Anchorage, AL 99510-1956

Tel: 907-566-2001

E-mail: Alaska@paralegals.org

ARIZONA

Arizona Association of Professional
Paralegals, Inc.

P.O. Box 430

Phoenix, AZ 85001

E-mail: Arizona@paralegals.org

CALIFORNIA

Sacramento Association of Legal Assistants

P.O. Box 453

Sacramento, CA 95812-0453

Tel: 916-763-7851

E-mail: Sacramento@paralegals.org

San Diego Association of Legal Assistants

P.O. Box 87449

San Diego, CA 92138-7449

Tel: 619-491-1994

E-mail: SanDiego@paralegals.org

San Francisco Association of Legal
Assistants

P.O. Box 2110

San Francisco, CA 94126-2110

Tel: 415-777-2390

Fax: 415-586-6606

E-mail: SanFrancisco@paralegals.org

COLORADO

Rocky Mountain Paralegal Association

P.O. Box 481864

Denver, CO 80248-1834

Tel: 303-370-9444

E-mail: RockyMountain@paralegals.org

CONNECTICUT

Central Connecticut Paralegal
Association, Inc.

P.O. Box 230594

Hartford, CT 06123-0594

E-mail: CentralConnecticut@paralegals.org

Connecticut Association of Paralegals, Inc.

P.O. Box 134

Bridgeport, CT 06601-0134

E-mail: Connecticut@paralegals.org

New Haven County Association of
Paralegals, Inc.

P.O. Box 862

New Haven, CT 06504-0862

E-mail: NewHaven@paralegals.org

DELAWARE

Delaware Paralegal Association

P.O. Box 1362

Wilmington, DE 19899

Tel: 302-426-1362

E-mail: Delaware@paralegals.org

DISTRICT OF COLUMBIA

National Capital Area Paralegal Association

P.O. Box 27607

Washington, DC 20038-7607

Tel: 202-659-0243

E-mail: NationalCapital@paralegals.org

FLORIDA

Florida Association of Paralegals, Inc.

12825 Harbor View Drive

Seminole, FL 33776

E-mail: Florida@paralegals.org

Tampa Bay Paralegal Association, Inc.

P.O. Box 2722

Tampa, FL 33602

E-mail: TampaBay@paralegals.org

GEORGIA

Georgia Association of Paralegals, Inc.

1199 Euclid Avenue NE

Atlanta, GA 30307

Tel: 404-522-1457

Fax: 404-522-0132

E-mail: Georgia@paralegals.org

HAWAII

Hawaii Association of Legal Assistants

P.O. Box 674

Honolulu, HI 96809

E-mail: Hawaii@paralegals.org

ILLINOIS

Illinois Paralegal Association

P.O. Box 452

New Lenox, IL 60451-0452

Tel: 815-462-4620

Fax: 815-462-4696

E-mail: Illinois@paralegals.org

INDIANA

Indiana Paralegal Association

Federal Station, P.O. Box 44518

Indianapolis, IN 46204

Tel: 317-767-7798

E-mail: Indiana@paralegals.org

Michiana Paralegal Association

P.O. Box 11458

South Bend, IN 46634

Tel: 219-237-1237

E-mail: Michiana@paralegals.org

Northeast Indiana Paralegal
    Association, Inc.

P.O. Box 13646

Fort Wayne, IN 46865

Tel: 219-424-7077

E-mail: NortheastIndiana@paralegals.org

KANSAS

Kansas City Paralegal Association

8826 Santa Fe Drive, Suite 208

Overland Park, KS 66212

Tel: 913-381-4458

Fax: 913-381-9308

E-mail: KansasCity@paralegals.org

Kansas Paralegal Association

P.O. Box 1675

Topeka, KS 66601

E-mail: Kansas@paralegals.org

KENTUCKY

Greater Lexington Paralegal Association, Inc.

P.O. Box 574

Lexington, KY 40586

E-mail: Lexington@paralegals.org

LOUISIANA

New Orleans Paralegal Association

P.O. Box 30604

New Orleans, LA 70190

Tel: 504-467-3136

E-mail: NewOrleans@paralegals.org

MARYLAND

Maryland Association of Paralegals

P.O. Box 13244

Baltimore, MD 21203

Tel: 410-576-2252

E-mail: Maryland@paralegals.org

MASSACHUSETTS

Central Massachusetts Paralegal

    Association

P.O. Box 444

Worcester, MA 01614

E-mail: CentralMassachusetts@

    paralegals.org

Massachusetts Paralegal Association

c/o Offtech Management Services

99 Summer Street, Suite L-150

Boston, MA 02110

Tel: 800-637-4311

Fax: 617-439-8639

E-mail: Massachusetts@paralegals.org

Western Massachusetts Paralegal

    Association

P.O. Box 30005

Springfield, MA 01103

E-mail: WesternMassachusetts@parale-

    gals.org

MINNESOTA

Minnesota Paralegal Association

1711 West County Road B, #300N

Roseville, MN 55113

Tel: 651-633-2778

Fax: 651-635-0307

E-mail: Minnesota@paralegals.org

MISSOURI

Kansas City Paralegal Association

P.O. Box 344

Lees Summit, MS 64063

Tel: 816-524-6078

E-mail: KansasCity@paralegals.org

NEW JERSEY

South Jersey Paralegal Association

P.O. Box 355

Haddonfield, NJ 08033

E-mail: SouthJersey@paralegals.org

NEW YORK

Long Island Paralegal Association

1877 Bly Road

East Meadow, NY 11554-1158

E-mail: LongIsland@paralegals.org

Manhattan Paralegal Association, Inc.

P.O. Box 4006

Grand Central Station

New York, NY 10163

Tel: 212-330-8213

E-mail: Manhattan@paralegals.org

Paralegal Association of Rochester

P.O. Box 40567

Rochester, NY 14604

Tel: 716-234-5923

E-mail: Rochester@paralegals.org

Southern Tier Association of Paralegals

P.O. Box 2555

Binghamton, NY 13902

E-mail: SouthernTier@paralegals.org

West/Rock Paralegal Association

P.O. Box 668

New City, NY 10956

Tel: 845-786-6184

E-mail: WestRock@paralegals.org

Western New York Paralegal Association

P.O. Box 207

Niagara Square Station

Buffalo, NY 14201

Tel: 716-635-8250

E-mail: WesternNewYork@paralegals.org

OHIO

Cincinnati Paralegal Association

P.O. Box 1515

Cincinnati, OH 45201

Tel: 513-244-1266

E-mail: Cincinnati@paralegals.org

Cleveland Association of Paralegals

P.O. Box 14517

Cleveland, OH 44114

Tel: 216-556-5437

E-mail: Cleveland@paralegals.org

Greater Dayton Paralegal Association

P.O. Box 515, Mid-City Station

Dayton, OH 45402

E-mail: Dayton@paralegals.org

Northeastern Ohio Paralegal Association

P.O. Box 80068

Akron, OH 44308-0068

E-mail: NorthEastOhio@paralegals.org

Paralegal Association of Central Ohio

P.O. Box 15182

Columbus, OH 43215-0182

Tel: 614-224-9700

E-mail: CentralOhio@paralegals.org

OREGON

Oregon Paralegal Association
P.O. Box 8523
Portland, OR 97207
Tel: 503-796-1671
E-mail: Oregon@paralegals.org

PENNSYLVANIA

Central Pennsylvania Paralegal Association
P.O. Box 11814
Harrisburg, PA 17108
E-mail: CentralPennsylvania@paralegals.org

Chester County Paralegal Association
P.O. Box 295
West Chester, PA 19381-0295
E-mail: ChesterCounty@paralegals.org

Lycoming County Paralegal Association
P.O. Box 991
Williamsport, PA 17701
E-mail: Lycoming@paralegals.org

Montgomery County Paralegal Association
c/o HRMML
375 Morris Road
P.O. Box 1479
Lansdale, PA 19446
E-mail: Montgomery@paralegals.org

Philadelphia Association of Paralegals
P.O. Box 159179
Philadelphia, PA 19102
Tel: 215-545-5395
E-mail: Philadelphia@paralegals.org

Pittsburgh Paralegal Association
P.O. Box 2845
Pittsburgh, PA 15230
Tel: 412-344-3904
E-mail: Pittsburgh@paralegals.org

RHODE ISLAND

Rhode Island Paralegal Association
P.O. Box 1003
Providence, RI 02901
E-mail: RhodeIsland@paralegals.org

SOUTH CAROLINA

Palmetto Paralegal Association
P.O. Box 11634
Columbia, SC 29211-1634
Tel: 803-252-0460
E-mail: Palmetto@paralegals.org

TENNESSEE

Memphis Paralegal Association
P.O. Box 3646
Memphis, TN 38173-0646
E-mail: Memphis@paralegals.org

TEXAS

Dallas Area Paralegal Association
P.O. Box 12533
Dallas, TX 75225-0533
Tel: 972-991-0853
E-mail: Dallas@paralegals.org

VERMONT

Vermont Paralegal Organization
P.O. Box 5755
Burlington, VT 05402
E-mail: Vermont@paralegals.org

VIRGINIA

Fredericksburg Paralegal Association
P.O. Box 7351
Fredericksburg, VA 22404
E-mail: Fredericksburg@paralegals.org

WASHINGTON

Washington State Paralegal Association

P.O. Box 48153

Burien, WA 98148

Tel: 800-288-9772

Fax: 253-813-9779

E-mail: Washington@paralegals.org

WISCONSIN

Paralegal Association of Wisconsin, Inc.

P.O. Box 510892

Milwaukee, WI 53203

Tel: 414-272-7168

E-mail: Wisconsin@paralegals.org

STATE AGENCIES OF HIGHER EDUCATION

Alabama Commission on Higher Education

100 North Union Street

P.O. Box 302000

Montgomery, AL 36130-2000

Tel: 334-242-2276

Fax: 334-242-0268

www.ache.state.al.us

Alaska Commission on Postsecondary
  Education

3030 Vintage Boulevard

Juneau, AK 99801-7109

Tel: 907-465-6741

Fax: 907-465-5316

www.state.ak.us/acpe/

Arizona Commission for Postsecondary
  Education

2020 North Central Avenue, Suite 275

Phoenix, AZ 85004-4503

Tel: 602-229-2591

Fax: 602-229-2599

www.acpe.asu.edu

Arkansas Department of Education

4 State Capitol Mall, Room 107A

Little Rock, AR 72201-1071

Tel: 501-682-4396

www.arkansashighered.com

California Student Aid Commission

P.O. Box 419026

Rancho Cordova, CA 95741-9026

Tel: 916-526-7590

Fax: 916-323-2619

www.csac.ca.gov

Colorado Commission on Higher Education

Colorado Heritage Center

1300 Broadway, 2nd Floor

Denver, CO 80203

Tel: 303-866-2723

Fax: 303-860-9750

www.state.co.us/cche_dir/hecche.html

Connecticut Department of Higher
  Education

61 Woodland Street

Hartford, CT 06105-2326

Tel: 860-947-1855

Fax: 860-947-1311

www.ctdhe.org

Delaware Higher Education Commission
Carvel State Office Building, 4th Floor
820 North French Street
Wilmington, DE 19801
Tel: 302-577-3240
Fax: 302-577-6765
www.doe.state.de.us/high-ed

Department of Human Services
Office of Postsecondary Education
Research and Assistance
2100 Martin Luther King Jr. Avenue SE,
Suite 401
Washington, DC 20020
Tel: 202-727-3688
Fax: 202-727-2739
www.dhs.washington.dc.us

Florida Department of Education
Office of Student Financial Assistance
1344 Florida Education Center
325 West Gaines Street
Tallahassee, FL 32399-0400
Tel: 888-827-2004
Fax: 850-488-3612
www.firn.edu/doe/

Georgia Student Finance Commission
2082 East Exchange Place, Suite 100
Tucker, GA 30084
Tel: 770-724-9030
www.gsfc.org

Hawaii State Postsecondary Education
   Commission
2444 Dole Street, Room 209
Honolulu, HI 96822-2394
Tel: 808-956-8207
Fax: 808-956-5156
www.hern.hawaii.edu/hern/

Idaho State Board of Education
P.O. Box 83720
Boise, ID 83720-0037
Tel: 208-334-2270
Fax: 208-334-2632
www.sde.state.id.us/osbe/board.htm

Illinois Student Assistance Commission
   (ISAC)
1755 Lake Cook Road
Deerfield, IL 60015-5209
Tel: 800-899-4722
www.isac-online.org

State Student Assistance Commission of
   Indiana
150 West Market Street, Suite 500
Indianapolis, IN 46204-2811
Tel: 317-232-2350
Fax: 317-232-3260
www.in.gov/ssaci/

Iowa College Student Aid Commission
200 10th Street, 4th Floor
Des Moines, IA 50309-3609
Tel: 515-281-3501
www.iowacollegeaid.org

Kansas Board of Regents
700 Southwest Harrison, Suite 1410
Topeka, KS 66603-3760
Tel: 785-296-3517
Fax: 785-296-0983
www.kansasregents.org

Kentucky Higher Education Assistance
   Authority (KHEAA)
1050 U.S. 127 South
Frankfort, KY 40601-4323
Tel: 800-928-8926
Fax: 502-696-7345
www.kheaa.com

Louisiana Office of Student Financial
   Assistance
P.O. Box 91202
Baton Rouge, LA 70821-9202
Tel: 800-259-5626 ext. 1012; 225-922-1012
Fax: 225-922-1089
www.osfa.state.la.us

Finance Authority of Maine
P.O. Box 949
Augusta, ME 04332-0949
Tel: 800-228-3734
Fax: 207-626-8208
TDD: 207-626-2717
www.famemaine.com

Maryland Higher Education Commission
Jeffrey Building, 16 Francis Street
Annapolis, MD 21401-1781
Tel: 410-974-5370
Fax: 410-974-5994
www.mhec.state.md.us

Massachusetts Board of Higher Education
Office of Student Financial Assistance
330 Stuart Street, 3rd Floor
Boston, MA 02116
Tel: 617-727-1205
Fax: 617-727-0667
www.mass.edu

Michigan Higher Education Assistance
   Authority
Office of Scholarships and Grants
P.O. Box 30462
Lansing, MI 48909-7962
Tel: 517-373-3394
Fax: 517-335-5984
www.MI-StudentAid.org

Minnesota Higher Education Services Office
1450 Energy Park Drive, Suite 350
Street Paul, MN 55108-5227
Tel: 800-657-3866
Fax: 651-642-0567
www.mheso.state.mn.us

Mississippi Postsecondary Education
Financial Assistance Board
3825 Ridgewood Road
Jackson, MS 39211-6453
Tel: 800-327-2980; 601-982-6663
Fax: 601-982-6527
www.ihl.state.ms.us

Missouri Student Assistance Resource
   Services (MOSTARS)
3515 Amazonas Drive
Jefferson City, MO 65109-5717
Tel: 800-473-6757; 573-751-3940
Fax: 573-751-6635
www.mocbhe.gov/mostars/finmenu.htm

Montana Office of Commissioner of Higher
   Education
Montana Guaranteed Student Loan Program
P.O. Box 203101
Helena, MT 59620-3101
Tel: 800-537-7508
www.mgslp.state.mt.us

Nebraska Coordinating Commission for
   Postsecondary Education
P.O. Box 95005
Lincoln, NE 68509-5005
Tel: 402-471-2847
Fax: 402-471-2886
www.nol.org/NEpostsecondaryed

Nevada Department of Education
700 East Fifth Street
Carson City, NV 89701-5096
Tel: 775-687-9200
Fax: 775-687-9101
www.nde.state.nv.us

New Hampshire Postsecondary Education
    Commission
2 Industrial Park Drive
Concord, NH 03301-8512
Tel: 603-271-2555
Fax: 603-271-2696
www.state.nh.us

New Jersey Higher Education Student
    Assistance Authority
P.O. Box 540
Trenton, NJ 08625-0540
Tel: 609-588-3226; 800-792-8670
TTY: 609-588-2526
Fax: 609-588-7389
www.hesaa.org

New Mexico Commission on Higher
    Education
1068 Cerrillos Road
Santa Fe, NM 87501
Tel: 800-279-9777
Fax: 505-827-7392
www.nmche.org

New York State Higher Education Services
    Corporation
One Commerce Plaza
Albany, NY 12255
Tel: 888-697-4372
Fax: 518-473-3749
www.hesc.com

North Carolina State Education Assistance
    Authority
P.O. Box 13663
Research Triangle Park, NC 27709-3663
Tel: 800-700-1775
Fax: 919-549-8481
www.ncseaa.edu

North Dakota University System
North Dakota Student Financial Assistance
    Program
600 East Boulevard Avenue, Department 215
Bismarck, ND 58505-0230
Tel: 701-328-4114
Fax: 701-328-2961
www.nodak.edu

Ohio Board of Regents
P.O. Box 182452
Columbus, OH 43218-2452
Tel: 888-833-1133
Fax: 614-752-5903
www.regents.state.oh.us/sgs

Oklahoma State Regents for Higher
    Education
500 Education Building
Oklahoma City, OK 73105-4503
Tel: 405-858-4356
Fax: 405-858-4577
www.okhighered.org

Oregon State Scholarship Commission
1500 Valley River Drive, Suite 100
Eugene, OR 97401-2130
Tel: 800-452-8807
Fax: 541-687-7419
www.ossc.state.or.us

Pennsylvania Higher Education Assistance
   Authority
1200 North Seventh Street
Harrisburg, PA 17102-1444
Tel: 800-692-7435
TTY: 800-654-5988
www.pheaa.org

Rhode Island Higher Education Assistance
   Authority
560 Jefferson Boulevard
Warwick, RI 02886
Tel: 401-736-1170; 800-922-9855
TTY: 800-654-5988
Fax: 401-736-3541
www.riheaa.org

South Carolina Commission on Higher
   Education
1333 Main Street, Suite 200
Columbia, SC 29201
Tel: 803-737-2260; 877-349-7183
Fax: 803-737-2297
www.che400.state.sc.us

South Dakota Board of Regents
306 East Capitol Avenue, Suite 200
Pierre, SD 57501
Tel: 605-773-3455
Fax: 605-773-5320
www.ris.sdbor.edu

Tennessee Student Assistance Corporation
404 James Robertson Parkway, Suite 1950
Nashville, TN 37243
Tel: 800-342-1663; 615-741-1346
Fax: 615-741-6101
www.state.tn.us/tsac

Texas Higher Education Coordinating Board
P.O. Box 12788, Capitol Station
Austin, TX 78711
Tel: 800-242-3062
Fax: 512-427-6420
www.thecb.state.tx.us

Utah System of Higher Education
355 West North Temple
#3 Triad Center, Suite 550
Salt Lake City, UT 84180-1205
Tel: 801-321-7200
Fax: 801-321-7299
www.utahsbr.edu

Vermont Student Assistance Corporation
P.O. Box 2000
Winooski, VT 05404-2601
Tel: 800-642-3177; 800-655-9602
Fax: 800-654-3765
www.vsac.org

State Council of Higher Education for
   Virginia
James Monroe Building
101 North Fourteenth Street
Richmond, VA 23219-3684
Tel: 804-786-1690
Fax: 804-225-2604
www.schev.edu

Washington State Higher Education
   Coordinating Board
P.O. Box 43430
917 Lakeridge Way
Olympia, WA 98501-3430
Tel: 360-753-7850
Fax: 360-753-7808
www.hecb.wa.gov

West Virginia Higher Education Policy
  Commission
1018 Kanawha Boulevard E., Suite 700
Charleston, WV 25301-2827
Tel: 304-558-2101
Fax: 304-558-0259
www.hepc.wvnet.edu

Wisconsin Higher Educational Aids Board
P.O. Box 7885
Madison, WI 53707-7885
Tel: 608-267-2944
Fax: 608-267-2808
www.heab.state.wi.us

Wyoming Community College Commission
2020 Carey Avenue, 8th Floor
Cheyenne, WY 82002
Tel: 307-777-7763
Fax: 307-777-6567
www.commission.wcc.edu

Appendix B

Additional Resources

For additional information on the topics discussed in this book, as well as helpful job-hunting information, refer to the following publications and online resources listed below. You'll also find a section of job descriptions from paralegal classified ads to give you an idea of the diversity of work available to a paralegal.

PUBLICATIONS

General Information

Bernardo, Barbara. *Paralegal: An Insider's Guide to One of the Fastest-Growing Occupations of the 1990s*. (Princeton, NJ: Peterson's Guides, 1997.)

Estrin, Chere B. *Everything You Need to Know About Being a Paralegal* (Albany, NY: Delmar Publishing, 1995).

Paralegals in American Law: Introduction to Paralegalism (Albany, NY: Delmar Publishing, 1994).

On the Job

Albrecht, Steve and Steve Albright. *The Paralegal's Desk Reference* (NY: Macmillan, 1993).

Black, Henry Campbell, Joseph R. Nolan, and Jacqueline M. Nolan-Haley. *Black's Law Dictionary* (Rochester, NY: West Group, 1991).

The Bluebook: A Uniform System of Citation (Cambridge, MA: Harvard Law Review Association, 1996) (Updated as appropriate).

Burton, William C. *Legal Thesaurus* (NY: Macmillan, 1992).

Faulk, Martha and Irving Mehler. *The Elements of Legal Writing: A Guide to the Principles of Writing Clear, Concise, and Persuasive Legal Documents* (NY: Macmillan, 1994).

LeClercq, Terri. *Expert Legal Writing* (Arlington, TX: University of Texas Press, 1995).

Association Publications

Publications from the National Association of Legal Assistants, Inc. (NALA)

The Career Chronicle (published by NALA annually) and *The National Utilization and Compensation Survey Report* (published by NALA biannually), which provide current information on the state of the paralegal profession.

Facts & Findings, NALA's quarterly journal, which contains educational articles for paralegals. Subscription is part of NALA membership.

Membership Newsletter, published at least quarterly to update NALA members on activities all across the U.S., including legislative and bar activities. Subscription is part of NALA membership.

Publications from the National Federation of Paralegal Associations, Inc. (NFPA)

Directory of NFPA Pro Bono Programs, with information on how individuals and associations can get involved in pro bono ("for the good"—legal services performed free of charge) causes.

NFPA Paralegal Compensation and Benefits Report, the results of an annual survey on salaries and benefits for paralegals. Also contains information on education, experience, and practice areas of paralegals.

National Paralegal Reporter, a quarterly publication provided to NFPA members. Past issues may be viewed on the NFPA website. (www.paralegals.org/Reporter/)

PACE Candidates Handbook, with sample test questions and an application.

PACE Study Manual

Paralegal Responsibilities, a booklet that summarizes the typical duties of paralegals in a variety of specialties.

Review Course for PACE Video

Publications from the American Association for Paralegal Education (AAfPE)

The Journal for Paralegal Education and Practice, a scholarly journal with articles by educators, legal assistants, and attorneys on issues affecting paralegal education and the paralegal profession.

Paralegal Educator, a quarterly magazine that features material on paralegal education, the paralegal profession, and AAfPE news.

Sidebar, a quarterly publication containing information on the activities of AAfPE and paralegal education in general.

Finding the Right College and Paying for It

Best 331 Colleges: 2001 Edition (Princeton, NJ: Princeton Review, 2001).

Cassidy, Daniel J. *The Scholarship Book 2001: The Complete Guide to Private-Sector Scholarships, Fellowships, Grants, and Loans for the Undergraduate* (Englewood Cliffs, NJ: Prentice-Hall, 2000).

Kaplan Guide to the Best Colleges in the U.S. 2001 (New York: Kaplan, 2000).

Occupational Outlook Handbook (Washington, DC: U.S. Department of Labor, 2000).

Peterson's Guide to Two-Year Colleges 1998: The Only Guide to More than 1,500 Community and Junior Colleges (Princeton, NJ: Peterson's Guides, 1997).

Peterson's Guide to Colleges for Careers in Computing (Princeton, NJ: Peterson's Guides, 1996).

The College Board College Cost & Financial Aid Handbook 2001 (New York: College Entrance Examination Board, 2000).

The College Board Index of Majors and Graduate Degrees 2001 (New York: College Entrance Examination Board, 2000).

ONLINE RESOURCES

Associations

Many of these associations have their publications online, as well as information about seminars and review courses for paralegal exams.

American Association for Paralegal Education	(www.aafpe.org)
Legal Assistant Management Association	(www.lamanet.org)
National Association of Legal Assistants	(www.nala.org)
National Federation of Paralegal Associations	(www.paralegal.org)

Other helpful links

Findlaw	(www.findlaw.com)
Gavel2Gavel	(www.gavel2gavel.com)
Internet Legal Resource Guide	(www.ilrg.com)
Katsuey's Legal Gateway	(www.katsuey.com)
Law Guru	(www.lawguru.com)
Legal Assistant Today	(www.legalassisttoday.com)
Legal Link Page	(www.hr.org)

Online Job Hunting

The Web is an extremely powerful job search tool that can not only help you find exciting job opportunities, but also research companies, network with other people in your field, and obtain valuable career-related advice.

Using any Internet search engine or portal, you can enter keywords such as: "resume," "paralegal jobs," "paralegal career," "paralegal job listings," or "help wanted" to find thousands of websites of interest to you. The following is a listing of just some of the online resources available to you.

Career-Related Websites

▶ Best Jobs USA—www.bestjobsusa.com

▶ 1st Impressions Career Site—www.1st-imp.com

▶ About.com—jobsearch.about.com/jobs/jobsearch/msubrespost.htm

▶ Advanced Career Systems—www.resumesystems.com

▶ America's Employers—www.americasemployers.com

▶ Career & Resume Management for the 21st Century—crm21.com

▶ Career Builder—www.careerbuilder.com

▶ Career Center—www.jobweb.org

▶ Career Creations—www.careercreations.com

▶ Career.com—www.career.com

▶ CareerMosaic—www.careermosaic.com

▶ CareerNet—www.careers.org

▶ CareerWeb—www.cweb.com

▶ College Central Network—employercentral.com

▶ First Job: The Web Site—www.firstjob.com

- ▶ Gary Will's Work Search—www.garywill.com/worksearch
- ▶ JobBank USA—www.jobbankusa.com
- ▶ JobSource—www.jobsource.com
- ▶ JobStar—www.jobsmart.org/tools/resume
- ▶ JobTrack—www.jobtrack.com
- ▶ Kaplan Online Career Center—www.kaplan.com
- ▶ My Job Coach—www.myjobcoach.com
- ▶ National Business Employment Weekly Online—www.nbew.com
- ▶ Salary.com—www.salary.com
- ▶ The Boston Herald's Job Find—www.jobfind.com
- ▶ The Employment Guide's Career Web—www.cweb.com/jobs/resume.html
- ▶ The Monster Board—www.monster.com
- ▶ The Wall Street Journal Careers—www.careers.wsj.com
- ▶ Vault.com—www.vaultreports.com/jobBoard/SearchJobs.cfm
- ▶ Yahoo Careers—careers.yahoo.com

Most of these sites list only jobs in the legal profession; however a few of them are more comprehensive. Use the search term "paralegal" to come up with a list of only those job openings that will be of interest to you.

Legal Employment Sites

- ▶ America's Job Bank (The Public Employment Service)—www.ajb.dni.us
- ▶ CareerPath*—www.careerpath.com
- ▶ Emplawyernet—www.emplawyernet.com (current charge is $9.95 per month)
- ▶ Federal Job Announcements—www.fedworld.gov/jobs/jobsearch.html
- ▶ Law Journal Extra—www.ljx.com
- ▶ Law Match—www.lawmatch.com
- ▶ Legal Employ—www.legalemploy.com
- ▶ NFPA—www.paralegals.org/center/StateEmploy/home.html
- ▶ Nonprofit Job Resource Center—www.nonprofitcareer.com
- ▶ Public Service Jobs—www.umich.edu/academic/opsp/jobsalert
- ▶ The Seamless Website Legal Job Center—www.seamless.seamless.com:80/jobs

*CareerPath lists ads from major newspapers, including the *Boston Globe*, *Chicago Tribune*, *Los Angeles Times*, *New York Times*, *San Jose Mercury News*, *Washington Post*, *Philadelphia Inquirer*, and *Southern Florida Sun-Sentinel*.

Appendix C

Websites for Paralegal Education Programs

At the time of publication, the websites listed here were current. Due to the dynamics of the Web, we cannot guarantee their continued existence or content.

Here you will find a list of popular and relevant websites from which to begin your search for a paralegal education program. Finding the right school and program is important, so be sure to make time for a serious investigation of each of site and their corresponding links to different programs.

In addition to the links found here, check with your state bar association, which usually will have information on paralegal programs. Most counties and cities have bar associations as well. Or check with a local paralegal organization that is affiliated with one of the national associations. For a complete listing of national organizations, state bar associations, and affiliated organizations of the National Federation of Paralegal Associations, see Appendix A.

www.paralegals.org

The National Federation of Paralegals Association, although not specifically recommending any particular school, provides a comprehensive Paralegal Education Program Directory. Organized by state, it lists names, addresses, and phone numbers of schools, with website and/or e-mail hotlinks to some. To find the list, select the "Getting Started" icon on their Homepage.

www.paralegalcolleges.com

A directory of colleges offering paralegal programs approved by the American Bar Association. They are arranged by state, giving the college name and town, with links directly to each school's website. The site also has a general directory of college names, arranged by state, with links to school websites.

http://stu.findlaw.com/schools/paralegal

This site provides a list of several schools in each state that offer a paralegal program. It has links to the school websites.

www.petersons.com

Peterson's College Quest program provides the opportunity for a personalized search through a database of thousands of colleges and universities. You can select a field of study, such as paralegal, then narrow the search by other criteria such as location and cost. A list of schools that meet your criteria will be displayed, providing detailed information about each school, including links to websites.

www.collegeview.com

This is another self-selecting search site, including over 3,000 colleges and universities. It includes information on each school and links to school websites.

www.embark.com

You can select your own criteria to search on this site which includes a business school section as well as colleges and universities. Detailed information and website links for each school are included.

www.xap.com

This personal criteria-based search site includes colleges, universities, and trade schools. The trade school section includes a number of schools with paralegal programs.

www.collegecenter.com

This site provides advice regarding the selecting of appropriate colleges and universities and free information about the admissions process, but it charges fees for specific guidance services.

www.rwm.org/rwm

A database of private post-secondary vocational schools. The viewer selects a state, then a field of training. The displayed list shows school name, address, and telephone number, and a link to the school's website.

www.universities.com

This site offers lists of over 7,500 colleges and universities, arranged alphabetically or by state. Includes detailed information on schools and links to their websites.

Each of the following sites provide names-only lists of colleges and universities arranged by state, with a hotlink to each school's website.

    www.collegescolleges.com; www.ecola.com/college;
    www.globalcomputing.com/universy.html;
    www.megamallandmall.com/college.html; www.ulinks.com

Appendix D

Sample Free Application for Federal Student Aid (FAFSA)

On the following pages you will find a sample FAFSA. Use this form familiarize yourself with the form so that when you apply for federal, and state student grants, work-study, and loans you will know what information you need to have ready. At print this was the most current form, and although the form remains mostly the same from year to year, you should check the FAFSA website (www.fafsa.ed.gov) for the most current information.

2001-2002

 **The FAFSA**

July 1, 2001 — June 30, 2002
Free Application for Federal Student Aid

OMB # 1845-0001

Use this form to apply for federal and state* student grants, work-study, and loans.

Apply over the Internet with  **FAFSA ON THE WEB**   **www.fafsa.ed.gov**

 If you are filing a **2000 income tax return,** we recommend that you complete it before filling out this form. However, you do not need to file your income tax return with the IRS before you submit this form.

If you or your family has **unusual circumstances** (such as loss of employment) that might affect your need for student financial aid, submit this form, and then consult with the financial aid office at the college you plan to attend.

You may also use this form to apply for **aid from other sources, such as your state or college.** The deadlines for states (see table to right) or colleges may be as early as January 2001 and may differ. You may be required to complete additional forms. Check with your high school guidance counselor or a financial aid administrator at your college about state and college sources of student aid.

 Your answers on this form will be read electronically. Therefore:

- use black ink and fill in ovals completely:
- print clearly in CAPITAL letters and skip a box between words:
- report dollar amounts (such as $12,356.41) like this:

Yes ⬤   No ⊗ ☑

| I | 5 | | E | L | M | | S | T |

$ | | 1 | 2 | , | 3 | 5 | 6 | **no cents**

Green is for students and purple is for parents.

If you have questions about this application, or for more information on eligibility requirements and the U.S. Department of Education's student aid programs, look on the Internet at **www.ed.gov/studentaid** You can also call 1-800-4FED-AID (1-800-433-3243) seven days a week from 8:00 a.m. through midnight (Eastern time). TTY users may call 1-800-730-8913.

 After you complete this application, make a copy of it for your records. Then **send the original of pages 3 through 6** in the attached envelope or send it to: Federal Student Aid Programs, P.O. Box 4008, Mt. Vernon, IL 62864-8608.

You should submit your application as early as possible, but no earlier than January 1, 2001. We must receive your application **no later than July 1, 2002.** Your school must have your correct, complete information by your last day of enrollment in the 2001-2002 school year.

You should hear from us within four weeks. If you do not, please call 1-800-433-3243 or check on-line at www.fafsa.ed.gov

 Now go to page 3 and begin filling out this form.
Refer to the notes as needed.

STATE AID DEADLINES

AR	April 1, 2001 *(date received)*
AZ	June 30, 2002 *(date received)*
*^ CA	March 2, 2001 *(date postmarked)*
* DC	June 24, 2001 *(date received by state)*
DE	April 15, 2001 *(date received)*
FL	May 15, 2001 *(date processed)*
HI	March 1, 2001
^ IA	July 1, 2001 *(date received)*
IL	First-time applicants – September 30, 2001
	Continuing applicants – July 15, 2001
	(date received)
^ IN	For priority consideration – March 1, 2001
	(date postmarked)
* KS	For priority consideration – April 1, 2001
	(date received)
KY	For priority consideration – March 15, 2001
	(date received)
^ LA	For priority consideration – April 15, 2001
	Final deadline – July 1, 2001
	(date received)
^ MA	For priority consideration – May 1, 2001
	(date received)
MD	March 1, 2001 *(date postmarked)*
ME	May 1, 2001 *(date received)*
MI	High school seniors – February 21, 2001
	College students – March 21, 2001
	(date received)
MN	June 30, 2002 *(date received)*
MO	April 1, 2001 *(date received)*
MT	For priority consideration – March 1, 2001
	(date postmarked)
NC	March 15, 2001 *(date received)*
ND	April 15, 2001 *(date processed)*
NH	May 1, 2001 *(date received)*
^ NJ	June 1, 2001 if you received a
	Tuition Aid Grant in 2000-2001
	All other applicants
	– October 1, 2001, for fall and spring terms
	– March 1, 2002, for spring term only
	(date received)
*^ NY	May 1, 2002 *(date postmarked)*
OH	October 1, 2001 *(date received)*
OK	For priority consideration – April 30, 2001
	Final deadline – June 30, 2001
	(date received)
OR	May 1, 2002 *(date received)*
* PA	All 2000-2001 State Grant recipients and all
	non-2000-2001 State Grant recipients in
	degree programs – May 1, 2001
	All other applicants – August 1, 2001
	(date received)
PR	May 2, 2002 *(date application signed)*
RI	March 1, 2001 *(date received)*
SC	June 30, 2001 *(date received)*
TN	May 1, 2001 *(date processed)*
*^ WV	March 1, 2001 *(date received)*

Check with your financial aid administrator for these states: AK, AL, *AS, *CT, CO, *FM, GA, *GU, ID, *MH, *MP, MS, *NE, *NM, *NV, *PW, *SD, *TX, UT, *VA, *VI, *VT, WA, WI, and *WY.

^ *Applicants encouraged to obtain proof of mailing.*

* *Additional form may be required*

STATE AID DEADLINES

Notes for questions **13–14** (page 3)

If you are an eligible noncitizen, write in your eight or nine digit Alien Registration Number. Generally, you are an eligible noncitizen if you are: (1) a U.S. permanent resident and you have an Alien Registration Receipt Card (I-551); (2) a conditional permanent resident (I-551C); or (3) an other eligible noncitizen with an Arrival-Departure Record (I-94) from the U.S. Immigration and Naturalization Service showing any one of the following designations: "Refugee," "Asylum Granted," "Indefinite Parole," "Humanitarian Parole," or "Cuban-Haitian Entrant." If you are in the U.S. on only an F1 or F2 student visa, or only a J1 or J2 exchange visitor visa, or a G series visa (pertaining to international organizations), you must fill in oval **c**. If you are neither a citizen nor eligible noncitizen, you are not eligible for federal student aid. However, you may be eligible for state or college aid.

Notes for questions **17–21** (page 3)

For undergraduates, full time generally means taking at least 12 credit hours in a term or 24 clock hours per week. 3/4 time generally means taking at least 9 credit hours in a term or 18 clock hours per week. Half time generally means taking at least 6 credit hours in a term or 12 clock hours per week. Provide this information about the college you plan to attend.

Notes for question **29** (page 3) — Enter the correct number in the box in question 29.

Enter **1** for 1ˢᵗ bachelor's degree
Enter **2** for 2ⁿᵈ bachelor's degree
Enter **3** for associate degree (occupational or technical program)
Enter **4** for associate degree (general education or transfer program)
Enter **5** for certificate or diploma for completing an occupational, technical, or educational program of less than two years

Enter **6** for certificate or diploma for completing an occupational, technical, or educational program of at least two years
Enter **7** for teaching credential program (nondegree program)
Enter **8** for graduate or professional degree
Enter **9** for other/undecided

Notes for question **30** (page 3) — Enter the correct number in the box in question 30.

Enter **0** for 1st year undergraduate/never attended college
Enter **1** for 1st year undergraduate/attended college before
Enter **2** for 2nd year undergraduate/sophomore
Enter **3** for 3rd year undergraduate/junior

Enter **4** for 4th year undergraduate/senior
Enter **5** for 5th year/other undergraduate
Enter **6** for 1st year graduate/professional
Enter **7** for continuing graduate/professional or beyond

Notes for questions **37 c. and d.** (page 4) and **71 c. and d.** (page 5)

If you filed or will file a foreign tax return, or a tax return with Puerto Rico, Guam, American Samoa, the Virgin Islands, the Marshall Islands, the Federated States of Micronesia, or Palau, use the information from that return to fill out this form. If you filed a foreign return, convert all figures to U.S. dollars, using the exchange rate that is in effect today.

Notes for questions **38** (page 4) and **72** (page 5)

In general, a person is eligible to file a 1040A or 1040EZ if he or she makes less than $50,000, does not itemize deductions, does not receive income from his or her own business or farm, and does not receive alimony. A person is not eligible if he or she itemizes deductions, receives self-employment income or alimony, or is required to file Schedule D for capital gains.

Notes for questions **41** (page 4) and **75** (page 5) — only for people who filed a 1040EZ or Telefile

On the 1040EZ, if a person answered "Yes" on line 5, use EZ worksheet line F to determine the number of exemptions ($2,800 equals one exemption). If a person answered "No" on line 5, enter 01 if he or she is single, or 02 if he or she is married.

On the Telefile, use line J to determine the number of exemptions ($2,800 equals one exemption).

Notes for questions **47–48** (page 4) and **81–82** (page 5)

Net worth means current value minus debt. If net worth is one million or more, enter $999,999. If net worth is negative, enter 0.

Investments include real estate (do not include the home you live in), trust funds, money market funds, mutual funds, certificates of deposit, stocks, stock options, bonds, other securities, education IRAs, installment and land sale contracts (including mortgages held), commodities, etc. Investment value includes the market value of these investments as of today. Investment debt means only those debts that are related to the investments.

Investments do not include the home you live in, cash, savings, checking accounts, the value of life insurance and retirement plans (pension funds, annuities, noneducation IRAs, Keogh plans, etc.), or the value of prepaid tuition plans.

Business and/or investment farm value includes the market value of land, buildings, machinery, equipment, inventory, etc. Business and/or investment farm debt means only those debts for which the business or investment farm was used as collateral.

Notes for question **58** (page 4)

Answer **"No"** (you are not a veteran) if you (1) have never engaged in active duty in the U.S. Armed Forces, (2) are currently an ROTC student or a cadet or midshipman at a service academy, or (3) are a National Guard or Reserves enlistee activated only for training. Also answer "No" if you are currently serving in the U.S. Armed Forces and will continue to serve through June 30, 2002.

Answer **"Yes"** (you are a veteran) if you (1) have engaged in active duty in the U.S. Armed Forces (Army, Navy, Air Force, Marines, or Coast Guard) or as a member of the National Guard or Reserves who was called to active duty for purposes other than training, or were a cadet or midshipman at one of the service academies, **and** (2) were released under a condition other than dishonorable. Also answer "Yes" if you are not a veteran now but will be one by June 30, 2002.

Page 2

Step One: For questions 1-34, leave blank any questions that do not apply to you (the student).

1-3. Your full name (as it appears on your Social Security Card)

1. LAST NAME	2. FIRST NAME	3. MIDDLE INITIAL
FOR INFORMATION ONLY	DO NOT SUBMIT	

4-7. Your permanent mailing address

4. NUMBER AND STREET (INCLUDE APT. NUMBER)

5. CITY (AND COUNTRY IF NOT U.S.)   6. STATE   7. ZIP CODE

8. Your Social Security Number

XXX – XX – XXXX

9. Your date of birth

☐☐ / ☐☐ / 1 9 ☐☐

10. Your permanent telephone number

(☐☐☐) ☐☐☐ – ☐☐☐☐

11-12. Your driver's license number and state (if any)

11. LICENSE NUMBER

12. STATE

13. Are you a U.S. citizen?
Pick one. **See Page 2.**

a. Yes, I am a U.S. citizen. .... ○ 1
b. No, but I am an eligible noncitizen. **Fill in question 14.** ...... ○ 2
c. No, I am not a citizen or eligible noncitizen. .... ○ 3

14. ALIEN REGISTRATION NUMBER

A ☐☐☐☐☐☐☐☐

15. What is your marital status as of today?

I am single, divorced, or widowed. ○ 1
I am married/remarried. ○ 2
I am separated. ○ 3

16. Month and year you were married, separated, divorced, or widowed

MONTH ☐☐ / YEAR ☐☐☐☐

For each question (17 - 21), please mark whether you will be full time, 3/4 time, half time, less than half time, or not attending. **See page 2.**

17. Summer 2001	Full time/Not sure ○ 1	3/4 time ○ 2	Half time ○ 3	Less than half time ○ 4	Not attending ○ 5
18. Fall 2001	Full time/Not sure ○ 1	3/4 time ○ 2	Half time ○ 3	Less than half time ○ 4	Not attending ○ 5
19. Winter 2001-2002	Full time/Not sure ○ 1	3/4 time ○ 2	Half time ○ 3	Less than half time ○ 4	Not attending ○ 5
20. Spring 2002	Full time/Not sure ○ 1	3/4 time ○ 2	Half time ○ 3	Less than half time ○ 4	Not attending ○ 5
21. Summer 2002	Full time/Not sure ○ 1	3/4 time ○ 2	Half time ○ 3	Less than half time ○ 4	Not attending ○ 5

22. Highest school your father completed — Middle school/Jr. High ○ 1   High school ○ 2   College or beyond ○ 3   Other/unknown ○ 4

23. Highest school your mother completed — Middle school/Jr. High ○ 1   High school ○ 2   College or beyond ○ 3   Other/unknown ○ 4

24. What is your state of legal residence?   STATE ☐☐

25. Did you become a legal resident of this state before January 1, 1996?   Yes ○ 1   No ○ 2

26. If the answer to question 25 is **"No,"** give month and year you became a legal resident.   MONTH ☐☐ / YEAR ☐☐☐☐

27. Are you male? (Most male students must register with Selective Service to get federal aid.)   Yes ○ 1   No ○ 2

28. If you are male (age 18-25) and not registered, do you want Selective Service to register you?   Yes ○ 1   No ○ 2

29. What degree or certificate will you be working on during 2001-2002? **See page 2** and enter the correct number in the box.   ☐

30. What will be your grade level when you begin the 2001-2002 school year? **See page 2** and enter the correct number in the box.   ☐

31. Will you have a high school diploma or GED before you enroll?   Yes ○ 1   No ○ 2

32. Will you have your first bachelor's degree before July 1, 2001?   Yes ○ 1   No ○ 2

33. In addition to grants, are you interested in student loans (which you must pay back)?   Yes ○ 1   No ○ 2

34. In addition to grants, are you interested in "work-study" (which you earn through work)?   Yes ○ 1   No ○ 2

35. **Do not leave this question blank.** Have you ever been convicted of possessing or selling illegal drugs? If you have, answer "Yes," complete and submit this application, and we will send you a worksheet in the mail for you to determine if your conviction affects your eligibility for aid.

No ○ 1   Yes ○ 3

DO NOT LEAVE QUESTION 35 BLANK

Step Two:

For questions 36-49, report your (the student's) income and assets. If you are married, report your spouse's income and assets, even if you were not married in 2000. Ignore references to "spouse" if you are currently single, separated, divorced, or widowed.

36. For 2000, have you (the student) completed your IRS income tax return or another tax return listed in **question 37**?

- **a.** I have already completed my return. ○ 1
- **b.** I will file, but I have not yet completed my return. ○ 2
- **c.** I'm not going to file. **(Skip to question 42.)** ○ 3

37. What income tax return did you file or will you file for 2000?

- **a.** IRS 1040 .... ○ 1
- **b.** IRS 1040A, 1040EZ, 1040Telefile ...... ○ 2
- **c.** A foreign tax return. **See Page 2.** ...... ○ 3
- **d.** A tax return for Puerto Rico, Guam, American Samoa, the Virgin Islands, the Marshall Islands, the Federated States of Micronesia, or Palau. **See Page 2.** ...... ○ 4

38. If you have filed or will file a 1040, were you eligible to file a 1040A or 1040EZ? **See page 2.**   Yes ○ 1   No ○ 2   Don't Know ○ 3

For questions 39-51, if the answer is zero or the question does not apply to you, enter 0.

39. What was your (and spouse's) adjusted gross income for 2000? Adjusted gross income is on IRS Form 1040–line 33; 1040A–line 19; 1040EZ–line 4; or Telefile–line I. $ ___,___

40. Enter the total amount of your (and spouse's) income tax for 2000. Income tax amount is on IRS Form 1040–line 51; 1040A–line 33; 1040EZ–line 10; or Telefile–line K. $ ___,___

41. Enter your (and spouse's) exemptions for 2000. Exemptions are on IRS Form 1040–line 6d or on Form 1040A–line 6d. For Form 1040EZ or Telefile, **see page 2.**   ___

42-43. How much did you (and spouse) earn from working in 2000? Answer this question whether or not you filed a tax return. This information may be on your W-2 forms, or on IRS Form 1040–lines 7 + 12 + 18; 1040A–line 7; or 1040EZ–line 1. Telefilers should use their W-2's.   **You (42)** $ ___,___   **Your Spouse (43)** $ ___,___

Student (and Spouse) Worksheets (44-46)

44-46. Go to Page 8 and complete the columns on the left of Worksheets A, B, and C. Enter the student (and spouse) totals in questions 44, 45, and 46, respectively. Even though you may have few of the Worksheet items, check each line carefully.   **Worksheet A (44)** $ ___,___   **Worksheet B (45)** $ ___,___   **Worksheet C (46)** $ ___,___

47. As of today, what is the net worth of your (and spouse's) current **investments**? **See page 2.** $ ___,___

48. As of today, what is the net worth of your (and spouse's) current **businesses and/or investment farms**? **See page 2.** Do not include a farm that you live on and operate. $ ___,___

49. As of today, what is your (and spouse's) total current balance of cash, savings, and checking accounts? $ ___,___

50-51. If you receive veterans education benefits, for **how many months** from July 1, 2001 through June 30, 2002 will you receive these benefits, and **what amount** will you receive per month? Do not include your spouse's veterans education benefits.   **Months (50)** ___   **Amount (51)** $ ___

Step Three: Answer all seven questions in this step.

52. Were you born before January 1, 1978? ....   Yes ○ 1   No ○ 2

53. Will you be working on a master's or doctorate program (such as an MA, MBA, MD, JD, or Ph.D., etc.) during the school year 2001-2002? ....   Yes ○ 1   No ○ 2

54. As of today, are you married? (Answer "Yes" if you are separated but not divorced.) ....   Yes ○ 1   No ○ 2

55. Do you have children who receive more than half of their support from you? ....   Yes ○ 1   No ○ 2

56. Do you have dependents (other than your children or spouse) who live with you and who receive more than half of their support from you, now and through June 30, 2002? ....   Yes ○ 1   No ○ 2

57. Are you an orphan or ward of the court or were you a ward of the court until age 18? ....   Yes ○ 1   No ○ 2

58. Are you a veteran of the U.S. Armed Forces? **See page 2.** ....   Yes ○ 1   No ○ 2

If you (the student) answer "No" to every question in Step Three, go to Step Four.

If you answer "Yes" to any question in Step Three, skip Step Four and go to Step Five.

(If you are a graduate health profession student, your school may require you to complete Step Four even if you answered "Yes" in Step Three.)

Step Four: Complete this step if you (the student) answered "No" to all questions in Step Three.

59. **Go to page 7 to determine who is considered a parent for this step.** What is your parents' marital status as of today?

(Pick one.) Married/Remarried ○ 1   Single ○ 2   Divorced/Separated ○ 3   Widowed ○ 4

60-63. What are your parents' Social Security Numbers and last names?
If your parent does not have a Social Security Number, enter 000-00-0000

| 60. FATHER'S/STEPFATHER'S SOCIAL SECURITY NUMBER | X X X – X X – X X X X | 61. FATHER'S/ STEPFATHER'S LAST NAME | F O R I N F O R M A T I O N O N L Y |
| 62. MOTHER'S/STEPMOTHER'S SOCIAL SECURITY NUMBER | X X X – X X – X X X X | 63. MOTHER'S/ STEPMOTHER'S LAST NAME | D O N O T S U B M I T |

64. **Go to page 7** to determine how many people are in your parents' household. ☐

65. **Go to page 7** to determine how many in question 64 **(exclude your parents)** will be college students between July 1, 2001 and June 30, 2002. ☐

66. What is your parents' state of legal residence?   ☐ STATE

67. Did your parents become legal residents of the state in question 66 before January 1, 1996?   Yes ○ 1 No ○ 2

68. If the answer to question 67 is "No," give the month and year legal residency began for the parent who has lived in the state the longest.   MONTH ☐ YEAR / ☐☐☐☐

69. What is the age of your older parent?   ☐

70. For 2000, have your parents completed their IRS income tax return or another tax return listed in **question 71**?

a. My parents have already completed their return. ○ 1

b. My parents will file, but they have not yet completed their return. ○ 2

c. My parents are not going to file. **(Skip to question 76.)** ○ 3

71. What income tax return did your parents file or will they file for 2000?

a. IRS 1040 .... ○ 1

b. IRS 1040A, 1040EZ, 1040Telefile ..... ○ 2

c. A foreign tax return. **See Page 2.** ...... ○ 3

d. A tax return for Puerto Rico, Guam, American Samoa, the Virgin Islands, the Marshall Islands, the Federated States of Micronesia, or Palau. **See Page 2.** .... ○ 4

72. If your parents have filed or will file a 1040, were they eligible to file a 1040A or 1040EZ? **See page 2.**   Yes ○ 1 No ○ 2 Don't Know ○ 3

For questions 73 - 83, if the answer is zero or the question does not apply, enter 0.

73. What was your parents' adjusted gross income for 2000? Adjusted gross income is on IRS Form 1040–line 33; 1040A–line 19; 1040EZ–line 4; or Telefile–line I. $ ☐☐☐ , ☐☐☐

74. Enter the total amount of your parents' income tax for 2000. Income tax amount is on IRS Form 1040–line 51; 1040A–line 33; 1040EZ–line 10; or Telefile–line K. $ ☐☐☐ , ☐☐☐

75. Enter your parents' exemptions for 2000. Exemptions are on IRS Form 1040–line 6d or on Form 1040A–line 6d. For Form 1040EZ or Telefile, **see page 2.**   ☐☐

76-77. How much did your parents earn from working in 2000? Answer this question whether or not your parents filed a tax return. This information may be on their W-2 forms, or on IRS Form 1040–lines 7 + 12 + 18; 1040A–line 7; or 1040EZ–line 1. Telefilers should use their W-2's.

Father/ Stepfather (76) $ ☐☐☐ , ☐☐☐

Mother/ Stepmother (77) $ ☐☐☐ , ☐☐☐

Parent Worksheets (78-80)

78-80. Go to Page 8 and complete the columns on the right of Worksheets A, B, and C. Enter the parent totals in questions 78, 79, and 80, respectively. Even though your parents may have few of the Worksheet items, check each line carefully.

Worksheet A (78) $ ☐☐☐ , ☐☐☐

Worksheet B (79) $ ☐☐☐ , ☐☐☐

Worksheet C (80) $ ☐☐☐ , ☐☐☐

81. As of today, what is the net worth of your parents' current **investments**? **See page 2.** $ ☐☐☐ , ☐☐☐

82. As of today, what is the net worth of your parents' current **businesses and/or investment farms**? **See page 2.** Do not include a farm that your parents live on and operate. $ ☐☐☐ , ☐☐☐

83. As of today, what is your parents' total current balance of cash, savings, and checking accounts? $ ☐☐☐ , ☐☐☐

Now go to Step Six.

Step Five: Complete this step only if you (the student) answered "Yes" to any question in Step Three.

84. **Go to page 7** to determine how many people are in your (and your spouse's) household.

85. **Go to page 7** to determine how many in question 84 will be college students between July 1, 2001 and June 30, 2002.

Step Six: Please tell us which schools should receive your information.

For each school (up to six), please provide the federal school code and your housing plans. Look for the federal school codes on the Internet at **www.fafsa.ed.gov**, at your college financial aid office, at your public library, or by asking your high school guidance counselor. If you cannot get the federal school code, write in the complete name, address, city, and state of the college.

	1ST FEDERAL SCHOOL CODE		NAME OF COLLEGE	STATE	HOUSING PLANS
86.		OR	ADDRESS AND CITY		**87.** on campus ○ 1 / off campus ○ 2 / with parent ○ 3

	2ND FEDERAL SCHOOL CODE		NAME OF COLLEGE	STATE	
88.		OR	ADDRESS AND CITY		**89.** on campus ○ 1 / off campus ○ 2 / with parent ○ 3

	3RD FEDERAL SCHOOL CODE		NAME OF COLLEGE	STATE	
90.		OR	ADDRESS AND CITY		**91.** on campus ○ 1 / off campus ○ 2 / with parent ○ 3

	4TH FEDERAL SCHOOL CODE		NAME OF COLLEGE	STATE	
92.		OR	ADDRESS AND CITY		**93.** on campus ○ 1 / off campus ○ 2 / with parent ○ 3

	5TH FEDERAL SCHOOL CODE		NAME OF COLLEGE	STATE	
94.		OR	ADDRESS AND CITY		**95.** on campus ○ 1 / off campus ○ 2 / with parent ○ 3

	6TH FEDERAL SCHOOL CODE		NAME OF COLLEGE	STATE	
96.		OR	ADDRESS AND CITY		**97.** on campus ○ 1 / off campus ○ 2 / with parent ○ 3

Step Seven: Please read, sign, and date.

By signing this application, you agree, if asked, to provide information that will verify the accuracy of your completed form. This information may include your U.S. or state income tax forms. Also, you certify that you (1) will use federal and/or state student financial aid only to pay the cost of attending an institution of higher education, (2) are not in default on a federal student loan or have made satisfactory arrangements to repay it, (3) do not owe money back on a federal student grant or have made satisfactory arrangements to repay it, (4) will notify your school if you default on a federal student loan, and (5) understand that **the Secretary of Education has the authority to verify information reported on this application with the Internal Revenue Service.** If you purposely give false or misleading information, you may be fined $10,000, sent to prison, or both.

98. Date this form was completed.

MONTH / DAY / 2001 ○ or 2002 ○

99. Student signature (Sign in box)

FOR INFORMATION ONLY.

Parent signature (one parent whose information is provided in Step Four) (Sign in box)

DO NOT SUBMIT.

If this form was filled out by someone other than you, your spouse, or your parent(s), that person must complete this part.

Preparer's name, firm, and address

100. Preparer's Social Security Number (or 101)

101. Employer ID number (or 100)

102. Preparer's signature and date

SCHOOL USE ONLY:

D/O ○ 1

FAA SIGNATURE

Federal School Code

MDE USE ONLY:

Special Handle

For Help — www.ed.gov/prog_info/SFA/FAFSA

Notes for questions 59–83 (page 5) Step Four: Who is considered a parent in this step?

Read these notes to determine who is considered a parent for purposes of this form. **Answer all questions in Step Four about them**, even if you do not live with them.

If your parents are both living and married to each other, answer the questions about them.

If your parent is widowed or single, answer the questions about that parent. If your widowed parent has remarried as of today, answer the questions about that parent **and** the person whom your parent married (your stepparent).

If your parents have divorced or separated, answer the questions about the parent you lived with more during the past 12 months. (If you did not live with one parent more than the other, give answers about the parent who provided more financial support during the last 12 months, or during the most recent year that you actually received support from a parent.) If this parent has remarried as of today, answer the questions on the rest of this form about that parent **and** the person whom your parent married (your stepparent).

Notes for question 64 (page 5)

Include in your parents' household (see notes, above, for who is considered a parent):
- your parents and yourself, even if you don't live with your parents, and
- your parents' other children if (a) your parents will provide more than half of their support from July 1, 2001 through June 30, 2002 or (b) the children could answer "No" to every question in Step Three, and
- other people if they now live with your parents, your parents provide more than half of their support, and your parents will continue to provide more than half of their support from July 1, 2001 through June 30, 2002.

Notes for questions 65 (page 5) and 85 (page 6)

Always count yourself as a college student. **Do not include your parents.** Include others only if they will attend at least half time in 2001-2002 a program that leads to a college degree or certificate.

Notes for question 84 (page 6)

Include in your (and your spouse's) household:
- yourself (and your spouse, if you have one), and
- your children, if you will provide more than half of their support from July 1, 2001 through June 30, 2002, and
- other people if they now live with you, and you provide more than half of their support, and you will continue to provide more than half of their support from July 1, 2001 through June 30, 2002.

Information on the Privacy Act and use of your Social Security Number

We use the information that you provide on this form to determine if you are eligible to receive federal student financial aid and the amount that you are eligible to receive. Section 483 of the Higher Education Act of 1965, as amended, gives us the authority to ask you and your parents these questions, and to collect the Social Security Numbers of you and your parents.

State and institutional student financial aid programs may also use the information that you provide on this form to determine if you are eligible to receive state and institutional aid and the need that you have for such aid. Therefore, we will disclose the information that you provide on this form to each institution you list in questions 86–97, state agencies in your state of legal residence, and the state agencies of the states in which the colleges that you list in questions 86–97 are located.

If you are applying solely for federal aid, you must answer all of the following questions that apply to you: 1–9, 13–15, 24, 27–28, 31–32, 35, 36–40, 42–49, 52–66, 69–74, 76–85, and 98–99. If you do not answer these questions, you will not receive federal aid.

Without your consent, we may disclose information that you provide to entities under a published "routine use." Under such a routine use, we may disclose information to third parties that we have authorized to assist us in administering the above programs; to other federal agencies under computer matching programs, such as those with the Internal Revenue Service, Social Security Administration, Selective Service System, Immigration and Naturalization Service, and Veterans Administration; to your parents or spouse; and to members of Congress if you ask them to help you with student aid questions.

If the federal government, the U.S. Department of Education, or an employee of the U.S. Department of Education is involved in litigation, we may send information to the Department of Justice, or a court or adjudicative body, if the disclosure is related to financial aid and certain conditions are met. In addition, we may send your information to a foreign, federal, state, or local enforcement agency if the information that you submitted indicates a violation or potential violation of law, for which that agency has jurisdiction for investigation or prosecution. Finally, we may send information regarding a claim that is determined to be valid and overdue to a consumer reporting agency. This information includes identifiers from the record; the amount, status, and history of the claim; and the program under which the claim arose.

State Certification

By submitting this application, you are giving your state financial aid agency permission to verify any statement on this form and to obtain income tax information for all persons required to report income on this form.

The Paperwork Reduction Act of 1995

The Paperwork Reduction Act of 1995 says that no one is required to respond to a collection of information unless it displays a valid OMB control number, which for this form is 1845-0001. The time required to complete this form is estimated to be one hour, including time to review instructions, search data resources, gather the data needed, and complete and review the information collection. If you have comments about this estimate or suggestions for improving this form, please write to: U.S. Department of Education, Washington DC 20202-4651.

We may request additional information from you to ensure efficient application processing operations. We will collect this additional information only as needed and on a voluntary basis.

Worksheets

Do not mail these worksheets in with your application.
Keep these worksheets; your school may ask to see them.

Worksheet A
Calendar Year 2000

For question 44 Student/Spouse		For question 78 Parent(s)
$	Earned income credit from IRS Form 1040–line 60a; 1040A–line 38a; 1040EZ–line 8a; or Telefile–line L	$
$	Additional child tax credit from IRS Form 1040–line 62 or 1040A–line 39	$
$	Welfare benefits, including Temporary Assistance for Needy Families (TANF). Don't include food stamps.	$
$	Social Security benefits received that were not taxed (such as SSI)	$
$ — Enter in question 44.		Enter in question 78. — $

Worksheet B
Calendar Year 2000

For question 45 Student/Spouse		For question 79 Parent(s)
$	Payments to tax-deferred pension and savings plans (paid directly or withheld from earnings), including amounts reported on the W-2 Form in Box 13, codes D, E, F, G, H, and S	$
$	IRA deductions and payments to self-employed SEP, SIMPLE, and Keogh and other qualified plans from IRS Form 1040–total of lines 23 + 29 or 1040A–line 16	$
$	Child support **received** for all children. Don't include foster care or adoption payments.	$
$	Tax exempt interest income from IRS Form 1040–line 8b or 1040A–line 8b	$
$	Foreign income exclusion from IRS Form 2555–line 43 or 2555EZ–line 18	$
$	Untaxed portions of pensions from IRS Form 1040–lines (15a minus 15b) + (16a minus 16b) or 1040A–lines (11a minus 11b) + (12a minus 12b) excluding rollovers	$
$	Credit for federal tax on special fuels from IRS Form 4136–line 9 – nonfarmers only	$
$	Housing, food, and other living allowances paid to members of the military, clergy, and others (including cash payments and cash value of benefits)	$
$	Veterans noneducation benefits such as Disability, Death Pension, or Dependency & Indemnity Compensation (DIC) and/or VA Educational Work-Study allowances	$
$	Any other untaxed income or benefits not reported elsewhere on Worksheets A and B, such as worker's compensation, untaxed portions of railroad retirement benefits, Black Lung Benefits, Refugee Assistance, etc. **Don't include** student aid, Workforce Investment Act educational benefits, or benefits from flexible spending arrangements, e.g., cafeteria plans.	$
$	Cash **received**, or any money paid on your behalf, not reported elsewhere on this form	XXXXXXXX
$ — Enter in question 45.		Enter in question 79. — $

Worksheet C
Calendar Year 2000

For question 46 Student/Spouse		For question 80 Parent(s)
$	Education credits (Hope and Lifetime Learning tax credits) from IRS Form 1040-line 46 or 1040A-line 29	$
$	Child support **paid** because of divorce or separation. Do not include support for children in your (or your parents') household, as reported in question 84 (or question 64 for your parents).	$
$	Taxable earnings from Federal Work-Study or other need-based work programs	$
$	Student grant, scholarship, and fellowship aid, including AmeriCorps awards, that was reported to the IRS in your (or your parents') adjusted gross income	$
$ — Enter in question 46.		Enter in question 80.— $